2020

R2SA Serviced Accommodation Book

ACQUIRE OPERATE **MARKET**

Agents and landlords have been burnt by inexperienced R2SA operators so entering the serviced accommodation market is not as simple as it was two years ago, and you won't make a fortune in seven days by simply using Airbnb and Booking.com; this book is an **eye-opener** for the newbies and a **game-changer** for those that are already operating. Learn new strategies to get more property at lower risk so you're more profitable and discover the online marketing tactics that no one is teaching so you can create a **real brand**, drive more **direct bookings** and **thrive**.

Disclaimer: Examples of financials, earnings or rents given in this book are not meant to be relied on as different factors determine how much profit a unit makes. ALWAYS do your own through due dilligence on any potential deal.

Contents

PREFACE 5

CHAPTER 1 12
WHAT IS R2R SERVICED ACCOMMODATION 12

CHAPTER 2 27
RESEARCH ON LOCATION: 27

CHAPTER 3 38
WAYS TO ACQUIRE A R2SA PROPERTY 38

CHAPTER 4 49
OPERATING YOUR SERVICE ACCOMMODATION 49

CHAPTER 5 73
MARKETING AND DISTRIBUTION OF PROPERTY 73

CHAPTER 6 101
DIRECT MARKETING STRATEGIES AND APPLICATION 101

CHAPTER 7 187
TAKE ADVICE BEFOREHAND, NOT AFTERWARDS. 187

FINAL THOUGHTS 195

RECOMMENDATIONS 199

Preface

The End of R2R Serviced Accommodation as You Know it

In the first edition of this book, back in 2018, before the Covid-19, before the enormous influx of everyone jumping into this widely promoted as an 'easy', 'passive' property investment strategy, I wrote: *"don t take it personally."*

I said: **"you cannot take it seriously when you are getting a barrage of abuse from guests, your personality has to be caring about the people you are serving."** That statement is even more relevant today. It's not getting easier to get in this property investment strategy, it's getting harder and if you haven't got thick skin, it will be very hard for you to get started, let alone survive.

At the time of writing this, the world is in a crisis caused by Covid-19, Insurance companies are not paying out, guests are cancelling and occupancy rates are in single digits, in fact, this is the worst time to be getting in hospitality and a lot of small operators will have to reduce their inventory or close down their companies because cash flow is king and when it's not present, with no idea when this crisis will be over, how do you confidently talk to your bank manager to increase, or establish a line of credit to get you through tough times? Everyone is trying to help one another but one thing we all know to be true is that 'help has boundaries, and it's not infinite. At some point, patience will run out and if you owe money, the door will be getting knocked on soon.

What I'm trying to say is business is tough, there is no '**easy** 'property investment strategy, you will make mistakes, some will be the nail in the coffin of your business, however, if you are the type of person who can fall, and then get up over and over again, you will go far in this business, as long as you are not greedy.

I am not the 'Rob Moore 'of property, I am certainly not a guru. I'm just a very hard working woman who has goals. I am qualified to write this book and give you insight because I have a small property portfolio now worth £1.3 million, I live a financially comfortable life, In 2018, I managed 80 R2R serviced apartments in 5 UK locations, 20 of those were operated under my brand and it's all thanks to the Rent-to-Rent serviced accommodation strategy. I had goals of growing to 100 units by end of this year (2020) but life happened and I changed direction. I am now content with what I have (12 apartment units and 3 luxury houses that I operate under my brands Welcome Apartments & My City Pod, PLUS I am a property manager of another 25 apartments for Investors and landlords), I consult for small and medium sized SA operators on digital marketing and day to day operational topics. With almost 10 years in the industry, I am positive that I can give you something to think about.

The R2R serviced accommodation industry is not as easy as it was two to three years ago to break into, landlords have become savvy in doing it themselves, some are just plain sceptical, agents do not really understand the model, they prefer an easy life of conventional tenants so the hard part is getting a good deal that's also **compliant.** If you manage to get a property, the hard part that awaits you is marketing it. Airbnb and Booking.com alone are no longer the cash cows they were back in the day. Increased competition, increased fraud meant a tightening of the belt by the OTAs, to the point where it's in my opinion unfair, mostly because it's inconsistent.

Can anyone tell me why booking.com decided to suddenly want a commission for cleaning fees? It's these types of restrictions, along with everything else that it makes it a false statement when property investment trainers say 'easy to make money from Airbnb and booking.com.' I will show you the figures later and then you can make your own mind up.

Look, don't get me wrong, I am in no way saying it's

impossible to make money from Airbnb and Booking.com alone, BUT if you're getting into SA via the R2R model, and you want to scale up so you can replace your 9-5 income, you will soon realise that within a year, the commissions and costs that come with this business will leave you working very hard, for very little. And whilst back in the day, I would have said "it's part of the game", today I am saying, you will burn out, you will lose money and you will be disappointed. Is there a way to actually make decent money and cashflow healthily? Yes there is, and in 2020 and beyond you have to get in the mindset that you are no longer in the business of running a serviced accommodation business, you are now in the business of marketing your serviced accommodation business; because everything depends on how well you are visible to the right guests, at the right time, with the right revenue management system in place.

The aim of this book is to take you through all of that before you pay for a train ticket to a free event with an upsell or before you, part with that £1,200 SA course with some type of mentoring. Mentoring is and will always be the most premium way to get ahead in any business, but it's a lot of money and time to spend just to realise it's not for you.

The last book I wrote on this topic was 52 pages long :(, actually, it's a 'guide', I made that pretty clear- this time, I have written an actual book. My writing style is conversational and straight to the point, no BS. There is no book like this on the market today and I doubt most trainers in their right mind would want to pack so much value in a £19.99 book but hey, I have always been a little bit crazy! The fact is that most of your peers are blind mice leading other blind mice. The proof is in the financial facts of every category of business, every profession, every sales organisation and every population. 1% create tremendous incomes and wealth, 4% do very well; 15% earn good livings; 60% stall, stagnate, and struggle endlessly; and 20% fail. Look at Fig P.1; working back up, you have an 80% poor and 20% prosperous ratio, a 95% vs. 5%, even a 99% vs. 1% ratio, thus, the overwhelming majority of your peers are engaged in business practices that fail them because they want to copy what someone else is doing. They are emotionally and intellectually committed about why you should follow the same path which often leads to frustration and failure. If you deviate and refuse or even dare to question the validity of this path, your peers, friends and sometimes business partners react violently. They criticise, they shame and shun. It's important to remember that every critic has his own agenda, whether conscious or subconscious. In writing this book, I am NOT saying you should copy me or anyone. You need to be intelligent enough to realise and understand that you have your own path to forge, perhaps I got here by luck, maybe it was hard work or a bit of both, but for you, it could be different. What I am saying is emulation is not the same as copying, and that's what most 'gurus' are selling. You cannot be the Warren Buffet of tomorrow without going through what Warren Buffet went through, chances are you never will, so be you, be proud of where you are and be aggressive about where you want to be three, six, one year from today.

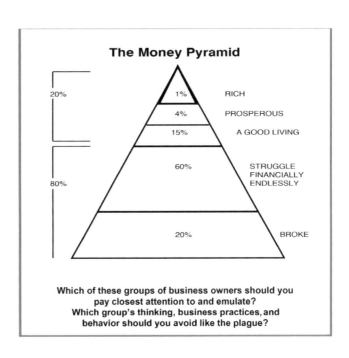

The Money Pyramid

20%	1%	RICH
	4%	PROSPEROUS
	15%	A GOOD LIVING
80%	60%	STRUGGLE FINANCIALLY ENDLESSLY
	20%	BROKE

Which of these groups of business owners should you
pay closest attention to and emulate?
Which group's thinking, business practices, and
behavior should you avoid like the plague?

ACQUIRE

Chapter 1

What Is R2R Serviced Accommodation

Objective: To find out what rent to serviced accommodation means and the types of guests you can have staying in your accommodation depending on your goals.

To put it quite simply, 'R2R serviced accommodation' is a property that's acquired via renting it from a landlord or agent, for the purposes of using it as a short term rental for the end user (the guest). Your profit is the difference you make after you've paid the rent and costs. This accommodation usually has amenities that are similar to a hotel such as housekeeping, and you can stay for one night or more. The biggest difference in what we do with our serviced accommodation is that we use properties like apartments, and entire houses whereas, a hotel offers their serviced accommodation on a room-by-room basis or a studio type of room. This book is going to focus on how to get into the serviced apartment business using the rent to rent method.

Up until a few years ago, the only way to get into this business was to either part with a huge amount of money in getting a commercial mortgage or signing a very expensive lease on a block of apartments. However, thanks to someone becoming creative, rent to rent was born.

The biggest benefit of getting into R2R SA in 2020 is that:

> **Low entry;** as you know buying a house means you need to pay a huge deposit upfront costing you at least £30,000 before you even think of furnishing it. With R2R, you literally pay one-month rent upfront and maybe a security deposit. Most savvy entrepreneurs use a company that insures your deposit which means you won't have to part with 4-6 weeks worth of rent tied up in deposits. Google 'Advanced rent deposit replacement insurance'. Give them a call and they will talk you through

requirements and the process. It's very simple and easy and is guaranteed to save you much-needed start-up capital. Think about it, if for example you live in Manchester and wanted to get into the serviced accommodation business, you'd only need roughly:

£900 for rent on a two-bed, grade B quality apartment in the city centre

£120 referencing fees

£1,350 security deposit (£200 if you use a deposit replacement insurance)

Total to acquire the property £2, 370

To buy a similar property would cost you at least **£180,000** and if you mortgage it, the minimum deposit you are looking at is £36,000 before solicitors fees and stamp duty.

What you are doing here with R2SA is making the same amount of money using someone else's property without parting with large sums of cash. Sure, when you buy property in the right area, you get the added benefit of equity gains of roughly 6% (give or take) every year, as well as the income; which is great if you have a lot of savings.

However, if you are new, and haven't got a lot of savings, the R2R model is the best way for you to get started in property investment. If you run your business like a real business, you should be able to recoup that initial investment within 6 months, depending on what time of the year you get started.

Tip: Do not get into SA during low season.

Occupancy rates are low, rates are low and it can prove to be quite catastrophic if you haven't got a decent line of credit in place.

Why serviced apartments:

The SA industry is now worth £150 billion worldwide. More and more travellers are increasingly using serviced apartments vs hotels mainly because of the added benefits that come with having your own spacious apartment vs a standard hotel room. According to HBAA, demand for serviced apartments is outstripping supply in many territories, due to:

- Greater adoption of serviced apartments in corporate travel policies
- More apartment operators taking short-stay business away from traditional hotels.

Growth in project and assignment work have shown that:

- 77% of business travellers stay in serviced apartments 5 times a year for up to 7 nights.
- Corporates choose serviced apartments due to cost per night, length of stay and location
- Of those who have stayed in a serviced apartment, 79% prefer them to hotels.

Using the Manchester example:

The average nightly rate for a 2 bed unit is £85 per night

The average occupancy rate for Manchester is 80% That's roughly £2,040 in monthly revenue

If your outgoings, including a 15% commission to online travel agents like booking.com is 60% of revenue, your operating profit will be around £816 per month!

This means, you can basically make at least £800 per month from property you don't own! And if you scale up to 4-5 apartments you could replace the income from your 9-5 working for someone else. How great is that?! The problem is, once you scale up, you are going to hit the VAT threshold soon afterwards so the best thing to do right from the beginning is to invest in getting direct bookings as soon as possible. Your aim is to reduce your guest acquisition costs from 15% to at least 9% AND increase your brand value, allowing you to charge more. As soon as you sign the lease to rent the property, stop thinking of yourself as just a serviced accommodation operator, start thinking yourself as a marketer of serviced accommodation. We will cover this in more detail in a later chapter.

Short-Term vs. Month-to-Month vs. Long-Term Rentals: Which One Is the Best?

Nailing down a viable business plan is a crucial first step for would-be short term rental operators. Some STR Operators prefer short-term rentals for high-profit margins with a high maintenance cost, while other operators stay with long-term rentals for a stable revenue stream, and some opt for month-to-month leases to get the benefits of both.

Which one is right for you? This section compares earning potentials, maintenance, tax benefits, and operational risks to help you make the most informed decision.

Take a look at the high-level summary first:

Short-term rentals

Short-term rentals have gained momentum in recent years as their flexibility allows travellers to rent anywhere from a few days to a few months. Short-term rentals, also called vacation rentals, are typically furnished apartments, condos, or houses where renters can feel more at home. Short-term rentals can be more appealing than hotels because of the prices, furnishings, and amount of space they can often provide.

	Short term	Month-to-month	Long term
Length of stay	3-7+ days	30+ days	1 year
Rent	£150	£120	£99
Occupancy	87%	95%	100%
Work needed	30+ hrs/ month	5-10 hrs/month	1-5 hrs/ month
Regulations	Strict in some cities	Flexible in most cities	Landlord/ tenant law
Flexibility	High	Medium	Low
Turnover	High	Medium	Low
Taxes	Corporation tax, standard VAT threshold	Lower VAT threshold, Corporation tax	Low VAT threshold, Corporation tax

Short-term rental benefits

There are plenty of benefits to owning a short-term rental. The top benefits to a short-term rental are the earning potential and flexibility.

Twice the rent of long-term rentals

Short term rentals can be lucrative—for the right time. If there a festival, sporting event or convention in town, you can easily double or triple your regular nightly prices. Operators can earn enough in one week to equal what a monthly rent would bring in.

Flexibility

You set fluctuating rates depending on your area's high and low seasons. Take advantage of the busy summer season to maximise your revenue, and lower your rates in the slow months to get more bookings.

Short-term rental hosts get to choose when to offer their space and for how long. You can easily block off your calendar or set the maximum stay length for your property. The added benefits of not having tenants for the long haul are fewer rental disputes.

Marketing is easy and brings quick results

Posting a property for rent is free on many short-term rental sites. However, since these types of rentals are incredibly popular, it is necessary to use good visuals and descriptions on postings for the property to stick out amongst the crowd.

Short-term rental challenges

At the same time, short-term rentals have downsides too, such as slow seasons, wear and tear from high turnover, and maintenance costs.

30-40 total hours 'work per month

Running a short-term rental take much more than creating a listing, if you plan to do it on your own. In fact, the reality of hosts is: Replying dozens of messages every day, waiting to hand the key to guests who are running late, washing the sheets, drying the towels, managing reviews, dealing with demanding guests. The list goes on.

Managing multiple listings is usually a full-time job. Even if you just have one listing, prepare to put in 30 to 40 hours ' work every month. Does it really take that much effort? Here's the breakdown:

Let's say your listing get booked 80% of the time, and you get 6 bookings a month for an average of 4 nights. For each booking, there's an hour to check-in and communicate with the guests, and another two hours to clean the property after move-out. That's already 18 hours a month.

If you get 5 guest enquiries and spend 5 minutes on each, that's half an hour a day, adding up to 15 hours a month. You probably need another two hours every month to update pricing and calendar and learn about the latest hospitality trends.

Short-term rental hosts are not only competing with thousands of hotel rooms in the city, but also more with their fellow neighbours as more people are getting into the business.

Occupancy rate varies greatly depending on the location, from 85% in London to just 60% in Bournemouth .

Even in the busy market of London, short-term rentals occupancy is much lower than long-term rental occupancy rates, which is almost 95%.

Changing regulations

With short-term rental regulations popping up across the country, it is imperative that Operators are well-versed in their area's regulations. These regulations are very local in nature and have complex clauses.

For example, London regulations makes it illegal to rent out an apartment on a short term rental basis for 90 days or more in a year. In fact, advertising such an apartment is not allowed after the 90 days. A hefty fine is imposed if you are caught by the local authority.

Think about short-term rentals as a hospitality business, rather than an apartment rental business. Hosts need to maintain great general upkeep of your property—from modern decorations to clean towels and even gift baskets— or you could receive some negative reviews. The high volume of guests coming through accelerates the wear and tear of your home.

In addition, because tenants come and go, all utility fees would need to be covered by the operator.

Month-to-month leases

Month-to-month leases are exactly what they sound like–an agreement to rent a space on a monthly basis with the ability to vacate the property with short notice.

These rentals provide hosts with the benefits of both short-term and long-term. Hosts deal with less turn-over than short-term rentals, and enjoy more flexibility than long-term rentals.

Month-to-month rental benefits

Less than 5 hours ˒work every month

Less turn-over means much less work for hosts. For the months that you send off old guests and take in new ones, it's probably two hours of cleaning and an hour of paperwork and check-ins. For the months without turn-over, little work is needed.

Other small tasks, such as updating your price and availability, calling for repairs, replying messages, usually take up another couple hours.

87% higher rent than long-term rentals

Landlords usually charge higher rent for on a month-to-month basis than long-term rentals to cover the risks. Analysts from Savills compared the rental price of monthly and long-term rentals in 8 major U.K. cities, and discovered monthly rentals are on average 87% more expensive than long-term rentals.

No need to deal with short-term rental laws

Most short-term rental laws only apply to stays of less than 30 days. Hosts who set their minimum stay length at 30 days don't need to worry about such laws (if you're not in London). In most cases, landlords sign a lease with the tenants.

With such an agreement, it is easier for landlords to give tenants notice that they need to move out. The ability to easily evict a tenant in a month-to-month lease is especially beneficial to landlords in the UK where eviction laws are strict.

Flexibility

When you rent out your property by month, the ability to increase rental rates that are comparable to others in the area is a huge plus compared to long-term rentals. You also enjoy the flexibility of short-term rentals, including blocking off your calendar for certain dates and updating price and house rules.

Month-to-month rental challenges

Lack of marketing channels

The market for month-to-month rentals is still relatively small, although the enforcement of short-term rental laws is converting more short-term rental hosts into this market. In- fact, reducing your rates and imposing a min stay could see you improve your bottom line in the two years post Covid-19. Mid term is now the new short term according to Rentals United.

Some may say besides SilverDoor and a few corporate housing websites, there's not much online platform for hosts to list their properties. This is not accurate, I have compiled a list of housing websites that cater for guests who stay at least 14+ nights.

Long-term rentals

Long-term rentals are the most common type of lease agreements. Typically a year long, these leases offer landlords a stable, steady rental income while minimising turnover.

Long-term rental benefits

Minimum work

While landlords have to cover the costs to maintain and repair their properties, that's about it for landlords' responsibilities. Often times, landlords also charge tenants for any damages they've caused to their property beyond normal wear and tear.

Tenants are typically responsible for cleaning and covering the utility bills that are used.

Long-term rentals are usually not furnished, however if you're in the STR business, it would pay dividends if you furnish your property.

Marketing is easy

Since turnover is low, there may not be a big need to market the space except once a year or even longer. Options for marketing these types of properties can include anything from Rightmove, OpenRent, Airbnb to social media postings on local pages, which are free to low cost.

Long-term rental challenges

Don't expect high profit margins

Long-term rentals have the lowest rent compared to short-term and month-to-month rentals. And a STR Operator faces many restrictions if he or she wants to raise the rent.

Because everything is written in the lease, an operator can raise the rent only when the initial lease expires, whether it's a one-year or two-year or multi-year lease, and with the advance notice.

Lack of flexibility

Operators need to have a solid reason to evict someone, and evictions can be costly and time-consuming. A report from All Property Management listed renting to the wrong people as one of the seven deadly sins of property management.

It is necessary that STR operators do thorough background checks on potential tenants to avoid being stuck for months on end with issues. Potential tenants should complete all application forms and allow operators to perform credit checks and background checks. Operators should put forth the effort to reach out to previous landlords, employers, and other references listed as part of the screening process, the report said.

Operators should also make sure that tenants can afford the rent by verifying their income. It's also a good idea to hire a lawyer and have them prepare the lease agreement to ensure there are no loopholes and to make sure the operator is in compliance with housing laws. Solicitors can also help in the event of any rental disputes, such as late payments. A lawyer/ solicitor can help spell out any fees and repercussions for late rent payments in the lease. Although it may seem like there is more work involved for long-term leases, there is a steady payout to be expected.

What's next?

Once you've decided which type of is the most suitable for your needs and goals it is time to ready the property for rent and start searching for the perfect guests.

Guest Types

Loyalty level indicates how likely they are to become repeat customers

Leisure guests- these guests usually travel in groups made up of friends or families visiting a location purely for leisure or tourism. They usually stay for 2- 5 nights.
Loyalty level: 3/10

Business travellers- these guests usually travel alone or as team of two to a particular location for the purpose of business for example, a sales manager who lives in Dublin could travel to Bournemouth every quarter to attend a HQ meeting. They usually stay for 1-7 nights. Business travellers are also known to extend their stay for an extra night for leisure. **Loyalty level: 8/10**

Corporate clients- these guests are usually made up of a corporate company who books your accommodation for their employees. Guests who stay with you could travel alone, or with colleagues. Corporate clients usually book your accommodation for 3 weeks to one year. **Loyalty level: 9/10**

Getaway travellers- these guests are usually made up of couples or a group of friends or family. They tend to visit luxury places or locations for a break or holiday. Your property has to be unique or be in a sought after location to attract these guests. Their stays range from 2- 14 nights depending on season. These guests tend to be affluent and expect a high standard of accommodation, which is reflected in the amount of money they're prepared to spend. **Loyalty level: 6/10**

Contractors- these guests usually travel in groups of two or more. The company they work for will usually make the booking for them. An example is a marine company HQed in Leeds sending a team of s8 contractors to London to work on site for 3 weeks but going back home at the weekends. **Loyalty level: 6/10**

Strategy and Approach before Investing

A well- designed serviced accommodation strategy will help you achieve your goals safely and faster by avoiding expensive mistakes. It's a clear and efficient path that takes into account current personal and economic circumstances; it helps with prioritising and allocating resources properly, whether it's time or money. It doesn't matter if you're thinking of acquiring one or one hundred serviced accommodation units, getting into short term rentals without a strategy will be like trying to use Google maps without an address. If you don't know where you are going, how will you get there?

Tips on defining your strategy and approach:

1) Start with the end in mind- What is your goal? Are you going after yield, value appreciation or a combined approach? The truth is, everyone goes into this industry because of the potential of high profits, however of you don't clarify exactly how much profit you want to be making, how are you going to know what to aim for? I have worked with a few SA investors and some will start this business because they want a sustainable profit in a complex market, some want to leave a legacy for the future and some simply want to make better returns compared to alternative property investment e.g. buy to let.

2) Know where you are NOW- Be realistic about where you are now in terms of money, time and industry expertise. Find out what is needed, what can you bring to the table and identify the gaps. So many times I've consulted with investors who went into it thinking one thing, but ended up with another. I had a client who invested £30,000 in acquiring seven, two bed apartments. His hope was to net £8k per month, but when he got the aprtments, then engaged with a management company 3 months down the line because he realised there was more to it than just having 'processes', he ended up settling for a net income of £4.8k after paying management fees.

Had he done his due dilligence and got realistic about his starting point, his approach would have been different.

3) Find an effective, logical path that's suited to current market circumstances and ensure it fits with your goals and starting point. Market forces define value and therefore, the results. If you get into the STR business in low season, or in a downward economy, expect to make considerably less than you would say if you start in high season. Alternatively, you could decide to go for a specific niche that would book your apartments despite the economic seasons. If you dont ackowledge your own situation and the direction of the market, you may find yourself being dragged along by a strong, unprofitable tide. The most successful serviced accommodation managers/ operators see opportunities rather than problems and follow a strategy that works in the circumstances.

Everyone wants rewards, especially those getting into serviced accommodation. Unfortunately the reality is it's not always possible to consistently make a huge profit throughout market changes without taking on RISK or EFFORT. Anything with potential profit and value is also a question of, and source of, both risk and effort. This is something I learned from my business mentor, and have realised through personal experience.

Chapter 2

Research on location:

Objective: this chapter is going to focus on explaining how to research on a location to find out if it's suitable to start a serviced apartment business. We're going to be talking about the tools for finding the best properties in your area and how to create your treasure map

I'm going to be showing you the specific tool that we will be using. This service isn't free... but it will make you tens of thousands if you use it correctly, so go ahead and sign up. It's generally £20-£99 per month for a single post code and around £150 for an entire region (multiple post codes). You can cancel your subscription after the first month if you like or when you're done with your rescarch.

This treasure map tool is essentially a platform that collects data on Airbnb + VRBO and their listings. You're able to use that data to analyse the revenue, the pricing, the occupancy rates, and things like that for any location. So we're going to dive a little deeper into exactly how to use this tool and I'll show you how useful it can be.

First, we're going to start with specifically what to look for when deciding where to start your serviced accommodation business.

1. What part of town has the highest revenue?

2. What type / size of properties are doing the best?

3. What's the average revenue per entire home

4. If you're in the 50th, 75th, or 90th percentile, how much will you be making during the on-season and during the off-season?

Okay, these are some of the metrics we're going to look at. Also, to be in the 50th percentile means the Airbnb listing makes more than 50% of the other listings. To be in the 75th, you make more than 75%, and 90th means your listing makes more revenue than 90% of the other Airbnbs in your area. Makes sense right?

Ready, lets's dive in!

Here is what the tool looks like

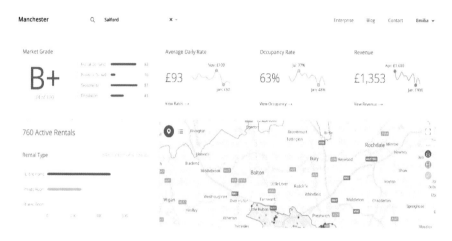

Go ahead and put your location in. In this book, we will be focusing on Manchester as an example.

This tool is called AirDNA and you can sign up for free to see what it's about. You only need to pay when you want to look at more detailed data about a specific location.

TIP: You can test it out fully by typing in "Nice, France" into the search bar.

The first thing you'll notice is that they give you a market grade in the area. You'll also get metrics like rental demand, revenue growth, seasonality, regulation. You can also see rental size percentages. For example, in this region, 46% of the rentals here are a single bedroom, and 25% are two bedrooms.

Going back to Manchester as a location, There's also a pricing section where you can see the average prices for each property based on size (number of bedrooms), post code, and revenue percentile. See figure below

But the most important section on AirDNA is the revenue tab. Here, you can see the revenue per month based on size, post code, and revenue percentile. In other words, I can discover the exact number of bedrooms and location that will make the most revenue. **See figure below**

Of course, the next step is to cross-reference these revenue numbers with the cost to rent properties in each post code. That is how we will find the most profitable properties (and it's not always the most expensive properties that make the most revenue so be careful!)

Here's an example.

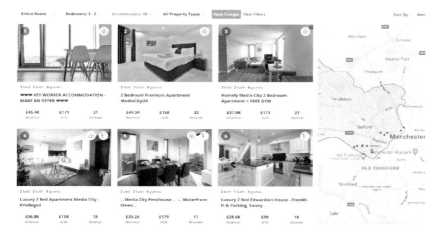

I don't use Airdna to cross reference the current rent for any particular location. I use Rightmove and Zoopla to get updated, current market rent details.

Looking at the Manchester example, properties in MediaCity seem to be making an average of £3,000 per month on Airbnb alone, See figure below

However, when you search on Rightmove, properties located in MediaCity seems to be averaging around £1,000pcm rent. See figure below.

But if you do your research properly, you'll find that properties just 6 minutes away form Mediacity, with a different post code in Salford also cost a lost less. See figure below:

Both these properties are in the 75th and 90th percentiles according to Airdna, but on different post codes.

Let's look closely at the figures. The first property is the expensive one in the prestigious MediaCity, the average occupancy for properties in the 75th and 90th percentiles is 90% with an ADR of £110/ night:

Revenue	£2,970
Rent	£1,155
Gross profit	£1,815

Then we find another zip code where the 90th percentile two bed-room properties are making on average £2,700 per month and the cost to rent on average is £750

Revenue	£2,700
Rent	£750
Gross profit	£1,950

Notice, how the revenue is less for the latter but the profit is greater. That's why this analysis is so important and it's not just about finding the highest revenue properties. It's about understanding the relationship between cost, revenue, location, and property size.

I hope you're starting to see how invaluable this tool is.

So you might be thinking, how do I make money just by

listing on Airbnb; because this tool only pulls data from Airbnb. Well, the good news is, if you have a location on Airdna and the occupancy rate for your chosen location is above 40% with a rental demand above 60%, your location will make a good investment. This is mainly because Airbnb is just one of tens of platforms you can list your property on. **Please see the figure below**

The biggest platform that will generate at least 70% of your revenue will be booking.com, however we will cover more on that in a later chapter.

Now that we've covered basic location financial research, we need to talk about guest/ market research.

Market research

Many people go into STR without even thinking about who they want to attract as guests. The location and property type you choose will determine what type of guests you have staying with you. If you choose a property. If you choose to acquire a property away from the CBD of a city, you are more likely to attract seasonal holiday makers and in some cases, relocating families. If you acquire a property in the CBD of a city, then you're more likely to acquire business travellers and party animals alike. How you brand yourself, and the pricing point you choose will determine who you attract as regular guests. Unless you are going into this business to host or cater for party guests, I suggest you position yourself in a location that will make it convenient for business travellers and corporate clients to stay mainly because they tend to be repeat bookers, which will reduce your guest acquisition costs. Corporate clients who have employees travel for business always look for specific details when booking accommodation. Here are some questions you should say yes to, if you want to attract more business clients.

Properties that attract business clients:

- **Easy transportation:** If there's a big conference hall, tube or train station nearby or trade fair venue in town, you can bet business travellers will want to stay with you. They are usually coming from at least 200 miles away so the ability to get to meetings and on a train back home will be seen as a definite advantage.

- **Restaurants, & Gyms:** Business travellers usually travel alone and sometimes they don't feel like cooking after a long day working on a project. If your property is near decent restaurants, bars and gym it will serve as a plus point for your business.

- **Peace and quiet:** After the hassle of traveling and the strains of working, business travellers need their sleep. Help them fall asleep faster by placing them in an apartment furthest from the busy street. In addition to noises, light from outside can be distracting. This is something you should look out for when you're viewing potential properties to invest in.

The above is a small sample of factors that could play into your decision. Your budget is another major important factor, and you may also need to look at: Local ordinances, foot traffic, utility costs, and so on.

The other bit of research you need to do is Competitor research. You need to make a detailed overview of your competition. We differentiate competitors in 2 groups. First we look at conceptual competitors that have a concept which is similar or comparable to yours in essence. And second, there are proximity competitors that are in your immediate surroundings and this will be your local competition.

Start with building a summary outlining in detail:

- hotel/ serviced accommodation name
- concept type
- number of rooms/ apartments
- star rating
- chain affiliation
- address
- area
- all facilities
- website url
- website languages
- website versions (desktop, mobile, tablet)

- online reputation and review scores
- price range and average rate (see Google Hotel Finder and TripAdvisor)

Add notes with anything that is unique about their operations, service that differentiates them from the rest. It will help you at a later stage defining a competitive strategy.

It would be good if you can get monthly performance data on the individual hotels/ STRs as well. You will gain valuable understanding of the seasonal fluctuations of the market.

Development Pipeline

What other hotels are planned to be constructed and open in your immediate area? How many rooms will be added? How will this impact your market share and financial results?

These are all very relevant questions that cannot be ignored. And investors will be extremely interested. Mind you, if an area is popular and many new hotels are planned it can have a positive effect as well, and increase overall demand.

Business Sources

What creates the demand in your market? Why do travellers come to your destination? What is the motive of their trip? Where are they coming from, or rather, what are you feeder markets? These are all questions that need to be answered. Your local tourist organisation or visitors bureau will have probably be able to provide you with valuable market statistics. But also go on the website of nearby airports, it will provide you with interesting statistics in terms of passenger data. You need to understand your sources of business and market segments to be able to make an effective marketing plan.

A classic example is STR companies usually want to enter the market with a flat rate structure. In essence from a positioning perspective it sounds great. You will attract a lot of consumer attention offering such transparency. However in reality, as hotel markets are driven mostly by dynamic rates which fluctuate with demand (a bit like the stock market), you will find your serviced apartment out-priced by competitors in low season

So, how to prepare and avoid these kind of situations? You will have to do a thorough market research and the above is good starting point.

Chapter 3

Ways to acquire a R2SA property

Objective: Finding out how to acquire a property via landlords and agents

Back in the day, it used to be a lot easier to acquire a R2R property. But the weird combination of landlords knowing that they can operate themselves, increased competition and smaller, new operators failing within the first year of business, it's become harder to get your first, viable property to use as SA. What you really want to make sure you do is that, you get a property at the right price, paying over the odds for a property means you will struggle to make the figures stack up. It's not enough to just call an agent and say you want a certain property to use for SA, you now have to show the agent or landlord who you are before they even decide to show you the apartment. As recent as just two years ago, agents and landlords were willing to take anyone on, as long as they had funds to pay for the property. These days, your reputation is just as important as your ability to pay. That's just the reality of getting started in SA in 2020, and I suspect it's going to get even harder.

So, here is the 5 step process I take through anyone I mentor regardless of whether they are going to use a Property Sourcing Agent, a letting agent or direct to landlord.

Step 1- Register a limited company; the name is not of great importance at this stage, however, avoid names that have the words 'investment' as this will raise flags because to be an investment type of company in the UK, you need to be FCA registered.

Step 2- Come up with a modern, non-chivvy brand name

AND secure the domain name as soon as you can. Make sure you check the name on the trademark website to ensure you can actually use it.

Step 3- Pay to get a logo and landing page designed. If you are not good at writing content, pay someone on Fiverr or PPH to write you a decent 'About us' column on the page.

Step 4- Show you're professional and get a phone number for your business and print some business cards.

Step 5- Open a business bank account and put any funds you have to start this business in there.

Once you have the above, you can start contacting sourcing agents, letting agents and landlords.

Ways to acquire a serviced apartment

There are 4 ways to acquire your first R2R serviced apartment. The way you choose to acquire the property depends on the funds you have readily available and the time you have to spend attending viewings

1. **A Sourcing Agent;** this is the quickest and easiest way to get your first serviced apartment; provided the agent is compliant, cares about you and has experience. There are many sourcing agents in property groups so if you contact them, ensure you tell them your requirements upfront. Whatever you do, DO NOT pay money for a property you haven't seen or signed for. Some sourcers will charge a small fee to start sourcing for you but before you part with

this fee, ensure you read their terms of service. If they haven't got terms of service, alarm bells need to be ringing. It's not enough that they are compliant or seem to be popular. You have to read their terms of service and sign an agreement with them that clearly outlines how long they have to find you a property, how much you pay upfront, is this upfront fee refundable, communication process between you and any potential landlords/ agents before the lease is signed! Should things go wrong, or should your circumstances change, you can fall back on the agreement instead of 'outing' someone in Facebook groups and losing any monies you've paid.

Speak and engage to at least 2 sourcers, that way you can ensure you have property offers being sent to you in a timely manner. Sourcing agents will usually charge based on the rent of the property AND the estimated turnover. So if we take the Manchester apartment as an example; an ethical sourcing agent should charge anywhere from £1,000- 2,500 per property.

2. **A Letting Agent;** with this option, you get to choose from a wide variety of properties, however, you may have to learn how to sell yourself before you even go to a viewing. Novices have a habit of arranging a viewing on the pretense that the property will be used for personal use, however, this practice does nothing but piss off the agent. You have to be upfront about who you are, why you want the property and how much you are going to be offering. That way the agent can be upfront with you

and let you know if it's even possible for you to have the property.

3. **Direct to Landlord;** This is by far the best option, however it just means you have to work extra hard. When you meet up and negotiate direct with the landlord, you have more opportunity to sell yourself and let the landlord know why it would benefit him to let you rent the property to you as a company vs. renting it to an AST tenant. You can find landlords on websites like OpenRent and if you want to go extra, you can run a local Facebook advert campaign that leads landlords back to your website/ landing page. That way, they can contact you with their details.

4. **Direct to developer;** this option is for those that have large capital behind them. When you approach a developer, it usually means you are looking to take on an entire block of apartments or a floor in a block of apartments. This type of arrangement this usually falls on is called a 'Master Lease'- this means you agree to be entirely responsible for the upkeep and maintenance of the building in exchange for rent. The benefits are you pay less rent than the market value, usually an average of 20-35% less; you have control over how you decorate the building and you have a much better chance of turning over a higher profit due to lower outgoings associated with these types of deals. If you are great at negotiating, you can get the block with no rent to pay upfront by asking to defer the rent for say 3 months. Security

deposits are usually lower because the buildings are empty shells. Word of advice- developers usually entertain these types of deals from reputable companies with a history in the industry, if you haven't got the history, then you need to have a healthy line of credit or funds to show that you are financially solvent. I have done three of these in my career and they have been the most rewarding financially. If you run your business well using this model, it's a lot easier to sell it on 3-4 years down the line as you're perceived to having a real asset in the lease, turnover and reputation.

Note to remember- Before you sign a lease or agreement, carefully consider the consequences should your business endeavor not go according to plan. It's not pleasant to think about the negative side of running a business, however every smart business owner should always have an exit plan, especially if you are starting something new. My advice is to always ensure you have a break clause that will allow you to give notice and leave the lease/ agreement should things not work out. Master leases tend to be a minimum of 5 years so ensure you have a 2- or 3- year break clause. Commercial agreements are usually a minimum of two years so ask for a twelve-month break clause. That way you and the landlord are both protected from negative any negative outcomes. Most people are almost scared to ask for a break clause because they think they might get kicked out just when things are going really well. The fact is there is no sane landlord who will want to get rid of you and leave the security of consistent rent coming in just to start marketing again and form a relationship with a new tenant.

Setting up your apartment

Let me tell you something, there is nothing more overwhelming and stressful in life than moving houses. So when you start the process of setting up your apartment, you need to mentally psyche yourself for the challenge ahead. Most gurus will tell you that it's easy, you just have to have a system and 'systemise', what the hell does that even mean? The reality is there will be a lot of work for you to do. If you don't do the work yourself then you are going to have to part with money to have somebody else do it for you. In my opinion, it's always better if you do the set up yourself the first time, that way you can create your own system for the next time. There are no shortcuts unless you have quite a bit of money, in which case you should be looking at a completely different property investment strategy.

Here is a list of essential things you should definitely think about when setting up:

1. **Furniture;** your apartment has to be fully furnished and fully equipped, and if you want quality guests and be able to charge more, the furniture has to be premium. You can either buy the furniture or you can 'rent' it. It all depends on the amount of funds you have available. If you are going to buy the furniture, my advice is to buy it on finance, that way you can buy exactly what you want, own it at the end

44

of the payment agreement, and write it off as an expense when it comes to doing your taxes. If you have good credit, it's also cheaper than renting/leasing the furniture. Furniture leasing is also a popular and viable way to furnish your serviced apartment, the tax benefits are there, however, the furniture is not owned by you.

Furniture rental also tends to be slightly more expensive than buying on finance, however, the benefits outweigh those of buying the furniture cash up front. David Phillips does really good furniture rental packages which range from basic to premium and depending on your budget, they can do a custom package. Whilst you're furnishing the apartment, you might also want to think about how you are going to sort the bedding and towels out. Again, the options are you either rent using a company like Stalbridge or you buy them wholesale using a company like Absolute Home Textiles. Just remember if you buy, it's your responsibility to wash and iron them. If you have one or two apartments, you can get away with buying and washing. If you have 3 or more apartments, hiring will be a less stressful option.

2. **Photographer**- please do not listen to anyone who tells you that you can get away with advertising your property with photos you take with your mobile phone. We are not in 2010 anymore when people used to get away with that kind of thing. Hire a professional photographer and get them to take photos in every angle possible, including the exterior and surrounding areas. Your apartment has

to be dressed or 'staged' to ensure a guest can imagine themselves in your property.

The photo is the most viewed on our website as it highlights much of the property in one shot: (living room, dining area, kitchen, master bedroom on the mezzanine level)

3. **Essential Insurance**; as a 'host' or 'operator' you need to have insurance that will cover you as an employer, public liability and for any damages that might occur as a result of having guests in your apartment. I recommend GuardHog or Alan Boswell. Be sure to tell the insurance company accurate information about where you advertise, the type of contract/ agreement you have in place and whether you employ people or not.

4. **Payment processing**; get yourself set up with a reliable payment processing company. Stripe, Worldpay and Barclaycard are the most popular and are aware of the serviced accommodation industry.

They will want to know your estimated turnover for the year and what percentage of it will be processed through their facility so make sure you have all this information ready to hand. It's highly recommended that you have a detailed business plan ready to hand. I use LivePlan.com for my business plans. It's simple and intuitive.

OPERATE

Chapter 4

Operating Your Service Accommodation

Objective: In this section we look at all the essential aspects of operating your serviced accommodation. Everything from cleaning to policies and channel managers.

Cleaning

Forget uncomfortable beds, poor service, or itchy bathrobes: serviced apartments' guests are most likely to be put off by poor housekeeping. Whether you run a cosy 3-star apartment or a five-star serviced apartment, guests never expect to be greeted by dirt, hair, or dust in their room, and complaints or negative reviews are understandable if this does happen. And, given that the majority of customers will read online reviews before booking an apartment these days, that can pose a real threat to your business.

Clearly, an effective housekeeping strategy needs to be a top priority for any operator. In this section, I'll show you how to properly clean your rooms and bathrooms, as well as share some tips for impressing your guests. This section will cover:

- What are the duties of housekeeping in a serviced apartment
- Creating a housekeeping strategy
- How to clean an apartment room: a step by step guide
- How to clean an apartment bathroom: a step by step guide
- Cleaning products, equipment, and supplies

What are the duties of housekeeping in a serviced apartment?

Good housekeeping is an invisible service, in that guests only really take notice of it when your team fails to deliver the expected standard of cleanliness. A serviced apartment could play host to hundreds of different guests each year, but no guest wants their room to feel used, which is why it's the role of your housekeeping staff to ensure that there is no evidence of any previous occupants, and that every room is completely clean from top to bottom.

On a daily basis, the housekeeping team is responsible for cleaning guest rooms and 'turning down 'beds, as well as replacing any dirty towels and replenishing any other amenities. On days when a bedroom needs to prepared for a new guest's arrival, an intensive clean and complete change of bedding will be required.

In addition to guest bedroom cleaning, some of your housekeepers should also be responsible for cleaning other front of house areas in the apartment, although generally there will be different teams and shift patterns for this.

Housekeeping teams are usually managed by a floor manager or supervisor, with a different manager overseeing each floor. They will usually be responsible for organising shifts, checking and inspecting the work of the housekeeping attendants, re-ordering supplies, and reporting any faults or problems with guest rooms to the relevant person.

Creating a housekeeping strategy

If you want your guest bedrooms to be as clean as possible, you'll need to have an effective housekeeping strategy in place. That means working out how many staff you need to employ per shift (depending on how many apartments you have) and creating a checklist for them to follow in each area to ensure cleaning standards are met.

It takes roughly 45- 60 minutes for a housekeeping attendant to completely clean an apartment, although it may take less time if only a basic turn-down service is needed. Assuming that a staff member works for eight hours (and allowing for a 30-minute break), they'll be able to clean around 4-6 apartments per shift, depending on the size of the apartments.

By dividing the total number of occupied rooms by 5, you should be able to work out how many staff members you need at a given time. Of course, this isn't representative of the total number of cleaning employees you'll need, as staff can't work every single day without a break, and you'll also need cover for holidays or sick leave.

How to clean an apartment: step by step

If your staff know exactly which steps to take from the moment they enter an apartment, it will help to stop anything from being forgotten or overlooked. That's why it can be helpful to provide your staff with a cleaning checklist they can follow.

I've put together two step-by-step guides for cleaning an apartment bedroom and bathroom, which you can use to create your own customised checklists. Remember, if you have different room types, you'll need to make different checklists for each one: the honeymoon suite is likely to have different cleaning requirements to your basic economy apartment, for instance.

To get a sparkling, five-star clean that will ensure your guests are happy with the standard of their apartment, your housekeepers should carry out the following steps in each bedroom before welcoming a new guest:

1. **Air out the room:** Before starting, open the windows and any balcony doors. This will help to bring fresh air into the room, and stops the smell of any cleaning chemicals from lingering. The housekeeping attendant should also leave the main door open while cleaning – this will help with ventilation.

2. **Strip the bed:** Remove bed linen and place it in the laundry bin in the housekeeping cart. If the room is occupied by the same guest for more than one night, they don't necessarily need a change of sheets, in which case the housekeeper should just neatly remake the bed and get the room ready for their return – this is called a 'turndown 'service. Some short term rental companies leave a card that the guest can place on the bed or doorknob to request a full linen change.

3. **Remove rubbish:** Empty the bins and remove any

rubbish from the room. Place new liners in the bins.

4. **Remove used cups:** Switch any used cups, mugs, or crockery for clean items, and replenish the hot drinks service (if any) with fresh supplies. Any items taken from the mini-bar should be noted and replaced according to the policy of your business.

5. **Dusting: Dust all surfaces**, starting from the top and working your way down towards the floor. Don't forget to dust any hard-to-reach or easy to miss areas, like light fittings, head boards, under the bed, or the top of wardrobes and cupboards. An extendable telescopic duster can be a very handy tool if your apartment has high ceilings!

6. **Vacuum furniture and upholstery:** Any pieces of upholstered furniture should be vacuumed using a specialist brush attachment. This will keep them free of dirt, dust, and allergens, as well as help to maximize their longevity. Curtains can also be vacuumed using an attachment to remove dust.

7. **Clean surfaces:** Clean and sanitise all surfaces. If any guest possessions are in the way, carefully move them to one side while you work, and then neatly replace them afterwards. Don't forget to also wipe down the insides of cupboards or wardrobes.

8. **Change the bed:** Inspect the mattress for any damage or wear. If no issues are found, place fresh sheets and pillowcases on the bed before making it up neatly in the style of your brand. Replace/ sanitise decorative cushions or throws.

9. **Sanitise and dust electricals:** Wipe and sanitise any electrical equipment like guest phones or televisions. TV screens can get very dusty, so wipe these with a dry cloth.

10. **Clean the floor:** By doing this last, you ensure that you aren't creating more work for yourself by making it messy again during other cleaning processes. Hard floors should be swept and mopped, while carpets should be vacuumed, starting from an inner corner and working out towards the door.

11. **Close windows and perform one last check:** Close the windows and any balcony doors. If any chemical smells remain, an air freshener can be used. If the thermostat has been adjusted, return this to your company's default temperature. Do one final sweep of the apartment to ensure nothing has been missed before the apartment is left.

Bathrooms tend to be much more prone to build-ups of dirt, mould, grime, and hair than the bedroom, so your staff need to be methodical and very thorough when cleaning this area. If you want to impress your guests, there shouldn't be any evidence that the bathroom has been used recently: it should feel completely clean and new.

For a hygienic, sparkling clean bathroom, your staff should follow this routine:

1. **Open any windows:** Open windows to allow fresh air in, or switch on ventilation units to help air out the room and stop the smell of cleaning products

from lingering.

2. **Remove towels and mats:** Soiled towels can be placed in the laundry bag. The usual protocol is to request that guests replace the towel on the rail if they wish to use them again, while dirty towels are placed in the bath or shower. If a guest wants to reuse their towels, put them to one side.

3. **Empty the bin:** Remove any rubbish and place a new liner in the bin.

4. **Tidy guest belongings:** Any toiletries or other products belonging to the guests should be neatly moved aside to allow for cleaning. These should be neatly replaced once cleaning has finished.

5. **Clean the shower and/or bath area:** Glass surfaces, tiling, and chrome shower fittings and taps should be cleaned using a specialist bathroom surface cleaner or glass cleaner to remove water marks and soap scum to create a shiny 'brand new' appearance. Pay special attention to the drain and be very careful to remove any hairs. If there is any standing water in the shower, report this to the floor supervisor, as it may indicate a more serious problem with the drain.

6. **Clean the sink area and taps:** Using an antibacterial bathroom cleaner and a cloth, wipe the sink and surrounding countertop. Clean the taps thoroughly to remove any water stains and provide a shiny finish. Wipe the mirror, being careful not to leave streaks or smears. Ensure the plughole is

completely clear.

7. **Clean the toilet:** The toilet should be thoroughly cleaned using a toilet disinfectant, and bleach should be applied and then flushed away. Pay close attention to underneath the rim and around the joints of the seat where grime and limescale can build up. Toilet freshening devices can be fitted to provide long lasting freshness. When finished, lower the seat and close the lid.

8. **Dust:** Dust light fittings and the corners of the ceiling to remove any cobwebs or dust, and clean behind and underneath towel rails and radiators. If any pipes are visible – behind the toilet or under the sink, for example – ensure that these are dusted.

9. **Wipe the towel rail:** This can accrue a surprising amount of dust and dirt, so don't forget to wipe it clean.

10. **Restock amenities and toilet paper:** Refill any used guest toiletries, such as shampoos, shower gels, soaps, or toothpastes. Restock any clean drinking glasses and toilet paper.

11. **Hang clean towels:** Finally, restock with clean towels and bath mats, as well as any robes and slippers if the old ones are soiled. If the guest has opted to re-use their towels, fold them neatly and re-hang on the towel rail.

12. **Clean the floor:** The floor should be swept or vacuumed, and then cleaned using a hard floor

cleaner and a mop. As with the bedroom, it's best to do this last, otherwise you may end up undoing your hard work by making a mess when cleaning other surfaces. Start from an inside corner and work outwards towards the door.

I felt it was important to write this much detail regarding cleaning because it's an area that's often overlooked. If you want to hire quality staff, use websites like Caterer and Indeed to advertise. My advice is request that all applicants have at least 6 months experience of cleaning hotels, care homes or hospitals (basically any hospitality, leisure or retail setting). This ensures that the cleaner has experience of cleaning to a high standard and can work well under pressure. Housekeeping teams deserve to be paid well so try and meet the Living Wage of your town. The last thing you want is to hire a good cleaner, but because you're paying too little, they leave for a better paying employee.

Emergencies

It's 10pm on a cold winter night, you've just settled on your sofa after a long day dealing with guests and admin work. The phone rings, and it's your guest frantic and screaming down the phone because there is no hot water and heating in the apartment. She's just come back from working late and needs heating, urgently! What do you do? Are you going to be reactive, or are you going to be proactive?

Emergencies happen all the time, but when they happen in your business, not only does it affect you, it affects your guest as well in a very inconvenient way. That's why it's very important to have a plan for any eventualities. Before you start trading, ensure you call around and engage with at least three local contractors in electricity, plumbing, heating and upholstery/ carpet cleaning. Speak to them, tell them your company name and what you do. Get a price and details of any call out fees and hours of business. That way, when a situation like above happens, you can confidently calm the guest down, reassure her that you have a solution and give her a timescale on when to expect the situation to be resolved. Guests are human too, they don't expect magic, but they expect clear and concise communication. It's also handy to have some sort of partnership with another STR provider in your building just in case the issue can't be easily rectified and you need to move the guest to a different apartment.

Processes and systems

All businesses have systems, and they are in place long before the doors are open. Just imagine opening a store without having a way to display the goods, help people purchase them, or tell people about them. It wouldn't stay in business long. The same goes for your short term rental. The good news is there is software that's specifically designed to help you manage each aspect of operating your short term rental. The software used is called Property Management Software (PMS). Most PMS systems allow you to feed it custom information so it works especially for you and your business.

You need essential systems for:

- **Managing reservations-** Reservation management processes differ from one product to another, as well as from one company to another. However, there are some important things regarding reservation management that any software solution must be able to help you with. Otherwise, reconsider whether it is the right software for you.

- **Change overs and routine maintenance-** This is the part, where you have to decide what happens when a guest checks out. Is the apartment cleaned after a check out, or is it cleaned when an arrival is coming? If you don't define these simple processes early on, it can cause many issues. Imagine if you have a departure and arrival on the same day but you haven't sent a cleaner to turn over the apartment? The same applies for routine maintenance; you need to define how often the apartment is inspected, everything from the TV to wifi to upholstery. That way you can ensure guests receive consistent service.

- **Handling guest issues and emergency management-** This is one of the most important systems to create. When guests have a problem, they need help immediately. To avoid a small problem turning into a huge issue, define how quickly you respond to issues and what way they are dealt with.

- **General communications-** The most efficient

communication occurs at a minimum cost in terms of resources expended. Time, in particular, is an important resource in the communication process especially in hospitality. For example, it would be virtually impossible for you to take the time to communicate individually with each and every guest about every specific topic covered. Even if it were possible, it would be costly. That's why you have to consider having a FAQ on your website, commission a telephone answering service that knows your business so they can provide answers to guests when they make first contact.

- **Tracking marketing and social media automation-** In the business world, marketing is the key to survival. If you fail to promote your serviced apartment brand effectively, you are basically wasting your time. Research and development are obviously important, but there will ultimately be no one to sell your accommodation to if you are not being exposed. However, marketing is something that requires due diligence and constant management. The best way to ensure your plans are proving profitable is to track them.

- **Collecting reviews-** Your apartment's online reviews can be of huge benefit to your business or a massive detractor, depending on how well you manage them. Customer reviews will appear in many places across the web including on your own website, online travel agents, and social media. They're going to be one of the most viewed pieces of content regarding your property, so you need to pay close attention to them. The most popular platforms for you to ask guests to leave reviews are Trustpilot, your website and Google.

- **Collecting payments and processing refunds-** Payment processing is an important part of a hospitality organisation and management. Knowledge about how guests prefer to pay can help to optimise your payment solutions, maximising bookings and profit margin. The ability to accept a variety of payment methods (for example QR code) in person at the front desk is important, as not all guests arrive with a pre-planned trip, or prefer to pay offline after booking online.

Policies and channel manager

A channel manager is a tool that will allow you to sell all your apartments on all your connected booking sites at the same time. It will automatically update your availability in real-time on all sites when a booking is made, when you close an apartment to sale, or when you want to make bulk changes to your inventory. Most decent channel managers will allow you to define certain policies like cancellations, patients and security deposits.

Thoughtful policies and procedures for your short term rental are your first line of defence against disagreements with guests and other awkward or upsetting situations.

A property lawyer/ solicitor will walk you through the

contractual basics, like your reservation policies, and ensure any legal requirements are covered.

However, the essentials can vary depending on your preferences, and other guidelines outline your processes and expectations. Here's an overview of policies and procedures you should consider.

Must-Have Policies and Procedures

Reservation policies generally cover three critical aspects of the rental process: deposits, payment options, and cancellations.

Deposits

There are different types of deposits that may be applicable to your property.

- Reservation or booking deposit (i.e. 30-50% of total): An initial payment required to hold a reservation that's due on booking. Generally, this money is then applied towards the overall rental fee or security deposit.

- Security or damage deposit (i.e. £200 or 10 percent of the rental fee, whichever is greater): Collected in case of damage to the property. If you have cause you can deduct from this deposit, although you should be prepared (with documentation and dated photographs) to justify your decision. Otherwise, this deposit should be refunded after the final inspection.

- Pet deposit (i.e. £200 or 10 percent of the rental fee,

whichever is greater): Collected in addition to the damage deposit in case of damage from pets. Because extra cleaning may be required whether there's damage or not, some owners charge a daily or flat-rate pet fee instead. (See below for information about an overall pet policy.)

Payments

In addition to detailing acceptable payment options, your payment policy also outlines when payment is expected – including any special fees – and any specific terms you've set. For example:

- Full payment is typically due before the rental period begins, so you can ensure any transactions clear and respond if payment is not forthcoming.

- You may set different guidelines depending on length of the reservation; short rentals may be payable on arrival, while longer rentals may be due a month in advance.

Acceptable payment can be anything from PayPal to direct bank transfer. However, instant cash (like Western Union or MoneyGram) is not advisable; it is too often connected to scams.

Cash itself is not ideal; it can't be sent by mail, and expecting it on arrival may leave you empty-handed; your options are limited if your renters show up without the amount needed.

Cancellation Policy

Cancellation policies vary widely and are often influenced by the local market. For example:

- Some properties provide a full refund if a reservation is cancelled well in advance – for example, 60 days or more before the reservation date.

- Closer to the rental day – within 60 days, for example – some properties will refund all but the reservation deposit while others provide no refunds.

- Some owners will provide a refund only if and when the property is re-booked.

To set a policy that fits your property, consider these questions:

- How long was the rental period, and how much notice did you receive?

- How likely are you to fill a cancelled booking, and within what time frame?

- Do you incur any costs from cancelled bookings (i.e. a penalty for cancelling linen rentals and cleaning services), and if so, how much of those costs can you recover?

Always account for your time and ensure you cover any losses – particularly from external service providers.

Should-Have Policies And Procedures

While not necessarily something you need to work into

your rental contract, these considerations define who you rent to and how your property can be used.

Minimum Stay

Typically, a minimum stay policy limits rentals to one week or longer in high season, and three days or longer during low and shoulder seasons. Assess what you're comfortable with, what suits your niche market, and what's typical for your area.

Minimum Age

Some owners set a minimum age to protect their properties from the damage that can come with graduation or college parties. These policies may dictate that any guests under the age of 25 must be accompanied by a parent or older guardian, or that the owner of the credit card used for the reservation must be over the age of 25.

Smoking

In many ways, a smoking policy is based on preference. However, you should also check both your insurance policy for any related clauses.

Pets

No pets, some pets, all pets? There are a number of things to consider when it comes to your policy on pets – including details, like permitted dog breeds, that may be dictated by your insurance coverage.

Special Fees For Events And Extra Services

Will you accommodate special events like hen dos'? Are there extra fees for large groups? What other services do you provide on request? Be sure to outline any requirements or fees that are particular to your property.

When Appropriate...

Some issues may not have direct financial implications, but they can still impact your business – or your reputation with the neighbours.

- Explain how you handle lost and found items.
- advise your renters of local noise regulations, including quiet hours.
- Parking can become an issue, particularly with groups travelling with more than two vehicles. Advise your renters of alternate parking options.

Channel managers- what are they?

A channel manager lets you easily manage your apartment's rates and availability distribution across various third-party sites simultaneously. Its function is surprisingly simple: you manage your bookings by changing prices, inventory and inclusions without having to change settings across multiple sites. It's efficient and reduces the risk of making an error.

Why Do You Need This System?

For many operators, a large percent of bookings come

from third-party websites, as these are the sites that continuously advertise. They also have a global reach, ensuring people can find your serviced apartment no matter where they are in the world.

Of course, you pay a fee or a percentage rate, as this is how the OTA sites make their money. However, the uptick in bookings more than makes up for this.

The disadvantage is that there are so many channels available: Expedia, Booking.com and Agoda are just a few. Even if you opt only to use a couple of them, you still have to change settings across multiple sites every time you get a booking on one of them. If you are in a particularly busy city centre location or it's peak season, you may spend hours every day making sure each site is updated, costing you time and money.

How Does a Channel Manager Work?

As soon as a booking is made on one site, the channel manager automatically updates all the other websites in real time. This reduces the likelihood of a double booking. Because the systems are entirely cloud-based, you don't have to have a computer running, and you don't have to download any software to access it. Instead, it functions entirely through your browser.

This is particularly uscful if you have multiple properties. It lets you update rates according to demand, and you can reduce prices even if you aren't at the property. Indeed, many of these channel managers have integrated Android or iOS applications, so you can use a tablet or smartphone to make changes on the fly.

What Do Different Channel Managers Offer?

Different channel managers offer different benefits. Some provide a complete property management and front office system, whereas others are much more basic. The one that you choose depends on your own needs and your current commitments to software.

If you have sofa beds or zip link beds, some software allows customers to purchase multiple beds across the room, so you can sell the room in different ways to maximise profit. Most automatically manage various tariffs you set for multi-night bookings, and they let you create bulk allocations and updates in the event you have group bookings phoned through to your business.

To save money and reduce potential hassles, look for options with a free help-desk/ support.

A fully comprehensive system also helps you manage your online reputation, letting you counteract negative reviews and incorporate social media interfaces to boost your profile on websites such as Twitter and Facebook.

Booking Engines

Booking engines let you offer additional services outside of accommodation. A good booking engine can help you set up parking, airport transfers and meals in addition to straight accommodation, letting you give guests a fully comprehensive stay. Marketing these extra services sets you apart on social media and the web.

Overall, a channel manager helps to increase revenue by

maximising the number of distribution channels you have and minimising customer dissatisfaction by keeping your room availability accurate across multiple websites. This ensures you can get on with the running of your serviced accommodation business without having to worry about constantly updating websites.

Key takeaways

MARKET

Chapter 5

Marketing and Distribution of Property

Objective: This chapter focuses on all aspects of marketing and distributing your property using the OTAs and direct marketing strategies for corporate clients.

Paul Revere purportedly rode through the streets ringing a bell and yelling "The British are coming!" And everybody lit their candles and lamps and paid attention. He'd have little effect today. That was then; this is now. We are immune to noise. It's even harder to get and hold attention just by making a lot of noise. If that worked, the marketers with the biggest bullhorns would always win and would stay on top forever, yet with increasing frequency little upstarts unseat longevity brands and category giants. Before Airbnb, the was booking.com, then after Airbnb, there was OneFineStay. The point is, these days, with all the resources that we have ready to utilise, you are never too small to make an impact in your industry.

In any and every business, you're actually in a number of businesses. Most businesses have many deliverables, not one. A dental practice may be in the teenage teeth-straightening business with products from traditional braces to Invisalign, but also in the implant business with the older generation. Each business is the same, and serviced accommodation/ hospitality is no exception. A quantum leap in revenue occurs when an entrepreneur differentiates deliverables from business and sees himself in the marketing business. In other words, as you operate this business, you have to see yourself first and foremost as being in the 'marketing of your short-term rental business' instead of just being a short term rental operator. When you are focused on the 'marketing' aspect, and the 'money' aspect of your serviced apartment you think, behave, and govern differently than when you think you are in some other business.

If you have plans to scale up and go from one to two to three or even 50 apartments, you may be excited at the notion of making more money, but the reality is more units may mean more revenue, but it also means more outgoings, and the two biggest single outgoings you will have are VAT (currently 20% of turnover) and your OTA commission costs of at least 15%. When I first scaled up, going from 4 to 12 units I was left deflated when the accountants showed me the balance sheet at the end of the tax year. That was when I realised that I needed to make a profound shift in how I ran the business. At the time all my OTA profiles were on 18% with booking.com. I had all my properties listed on Expedia and LateRooms as well as SilverDoor but those commission fees where killing me! I was working way too hard and spending way too much time away from home just to be netting £5k/ month. There was nothing I could do about the VAT (or so I thought) but I knew I could try and reduce the guest acquisition costs from 15-18% to at least 10%. I had to stop being lazy by letting OTAs like BDC take such a large chunk of my money so I went and got mentored by one of the best marketers in the world (Frank Kern), but it wasn't enough to learn how to just market, I wanted to learn how to apply that knowledge in the Travel/ Accommodation vertical. It cost me time and money but it was worth it. I started running Google ads, I was prospecting on Facebook and to start with, I didn't see any positive results, just a bunch of clicks and email sign ups, but as I kept tweaking and changing strategies, finally, the results started coming in. I had figured out a way to turn Facebook email sign ups to booking enquires, then actual confirmed bookings. I was also simultaneously running Google ads which meant I was getting a good mix of last-minute bookings and booking requests with a lead time of 14-30 days! It was great! But when I looked at the amount of money I had spent over those 6 months, I had spent a lot more than 18%. After looking at it with my mentor, we realised that we couldn't fulfil 40% of booking requests that came in because we had no availability, however we were still being charged for the clicks. My mentor advised to change strategy. Instead of spending money on acquiring new guests, he suggested that I spent 60% of the online marketing budget on producing repeat customers from the guests that had already stayed. But also, instead of focusing on leisure guests, I should focus on business guests. That quarter, the results where nothing short of amazing. The acquisition costs had gone down to 9%, VAT had reduced because some the apartments had guests staying for 28+ nights from the same company so instead of it being 20%, it went down to 4%

Here is an example breakdown of how it worked:

Deloitte India (our guest) has a team of 16 project managers who come to the UK regularly.

We charge them £99/ night instead of £150 in London for 90 days booking

Their project managers come to stay between 14 and 30 nights

When there's a departure, we service the apartment at an

extra fee of £40

The reduced rate of VAT kicks in because we have the same guest (Deloitte) staying for more than 28 consecutive nights. No breaks.

There is no £0 acquisition costs

This arrangement lasted a total of 6 months, not only with Deloitte, but with other companies as well, both in the UK and in abroad. With a small portfolio of 12, all we needed was a handful of companies who use us regularly for accommodation. We reduced our online marketing budget considerably and focused on 'direct marketing'- which I will explain in a later section of this segment. With this marketing strategy in place, I was able to scale up and take on more units using different lease models.

Without wasting too much time, lets's get to the next section.

Pricing and revenue management

There are a number of definitions and it does vary slightly from industry to industry, but with respect to hotels/serviced apartments the function of revenue management is to anticipate the demand for sales so that pricing and inventory management techniques can be applied to maximise yield.

Huh?

That definition might be fine if you are a dictionary, however we are not interested in vague management speak here, so what does this really mean. Well, revenue management basically aims to **maximise your revenue by "selling the right product (apartment), at the right time, at the right price to the right guest**." Essentially making sure you price your apartments at just the right price to give you the maximum revenue per room whilst also aiming for maximum occupancy levels.

Where did Revenue Management come from?

The Airline Industry is most often credited with the popularisation of Revenue Management, although it has been studied by economics professors in universities the world over for many years in various forms. We are all aware that you can book the same ticket on the same airline flight with the same company, but pay vastly different amounts of money depending on the time of day, day of the week and time of year of that flight as well as when you make the booking. This is not just random chance. The Airline Industry has carefully worked out at what price different segments of people (corporate travellers, families, students etc) will pay for their flight and what that demand will look like at different times of the day and days of the year and it makes sure that each plane is as full as it can be with people paying at each pricing level.

Revenue management is still fairly new in the hospitality industry and has only risen to prominence in the last 10 years. However, its rise to acceptance has been phenomenal, now with many medium to large operators having a dedicated Revenue Manager in place which is considered a senior management role.

During the mid-2000's the hospitality industry globally reported some pretty spectacular gains in Revenue per Available Room (RevPAR - more on this later). Much of this success had to do with a favourable economic situation - everyone felt like they had lots of money - but a great deal of this also had to do with the fact that this period saw the introduction of revenue management to the hospitality sector.

Ironically, from 2008 when things went globally and spectacularly wrong economically speaking, it was the revenue management practices developed in this period to which many industries turned to save them from ruin. When the number of people visiting your apartment suddenly and dramatically drops you had better make sure that you are making the most of the ones who are still coming!

Basic Revenue Management

That's enough of the history lesson. Hopefully I have now given you a hint of an understanding of the concept of Revenue Management and as we are all about giving you value and not just a history lesson, here are some simplistic revenue management strategies. Bear in mind that these are the most simple strategies, this is where you should start if you are not doing any form or revenue management at all, but do not dismiss this section of the chapter if you are already familiar with revenue management. We want to start at the beginning for those that are new to all this, but things are going to get a lot more interesting as we delve a little deeper.

Dynamic Pricing

The most basic form of revenue management deals with price and volume. You have a fixed number of apartments that you can sell at any one time (volume). You yourself can not easily increase the real demand for apartments in your area, but we all know there is a relationship between the level of demand and the price of something (if something is cheaper you are more likely to buy) so you can artificially boost the demand for your apartments by selling at a more attractive price. The key here is to make sure that you only sell those apartments at a lower price to those people that wouldn't normally have booked with you otherwise. Remember that there will always be people prepared to pay your standard rate and others who will be prepared to pay a premium rate, the whole idea of revenue management here is that you only sell the cheaper apartments to those people that would not have otherwise booked. Then to sell those apartments to the people willing to pay normal price at that normal price while also still selling the apartments at a premium to those who are happy to pay more. The most simple way to do this is to link your rates (prices) to the occupancy level (volume) of your apartment at any one time. Here is an example:- Let's say that in three months time you notice that you only have a few bookings in your business constituting approximately 15% occupancy. Now, you know that over the next few months you are sure to get some bookings that come in, but you want to make sure that as many of those people looking for accommodation in your area come to stay with you. So you implement a pricing system whereby you reduce your room prices by 15% until your business for that period reaches 30% occupancy. Then you only reduce your standard rates by 10% until you reach 40% occupancy. Your rates then revert to normal until you hit 70% occupancy and then your rates actually increase by 10% until you hit 90% occupancy. Any bookings over that level incur a 20% premium over your standard pricing. By doing this you are ensuring, all be it not very scientifically, that initially bookings are coming to you because you are offering a price incentive. Then as the level of of occupancy increases that price incentive reduces. Up to the point where your highest demand clients (i.e. late bookers and those that would be willing to pay whatever price) pay a premium to secure one of the last rooms available. If you are wondering which would make you better off, leaving your prices fixed versus flexing them as in the example above, well assuming in both situations that your apartments becomes fully booked then you are marginally better off with the above Flexible Pricing example. However, the point here is that you are attracting the right people at the right price at each pricing level, thus maximising your occupancy levels all the while maximising the rate that each person is willing to pay. Now this is a simple example and each business is going to be slightly different in terms of the point at which the prices should "flex" but this should give you a simple idea of what you can do.

My Top 5 Tips for getting people to book YOUR apartment!

These tips are designed for anywhere that people can find information about your business on line, but they still apply to wherever people can find information about your apartment, be that in magazines, leaflets or adverts.

1. **Keep It Simple –** Try not to have more than 5 Room Types available to your clients. Too much of a selection actually reduces the ability for people to make a decision. Equally people do not want just one option. Research has shown that 3 options is the optimal offering, but between 2 and 5 is reasonable.

2. **Have a "Superior" Apartment option** - Did you know that rooms with the word "Superior" in their name are the best selling rooms in the world! The great thing is that "superior" is subjective so it can apply to any premium offering. People will select it first and/or pay a premium for any room with "Superior" in the name so make sure you have one if you don't already.

3. **Practice Rate Parity –** People get confused when there are multiple rates on offer across multiple platforms. People do like to think they have "bagged a bargain" but too many price variations will actually put people off as they perceive the product at a lower value. Have the same price for the same room across all of your sales platforms so you don't confuse people.

4. **Paint a Picture** - Make sure your apartment descriptions are concise, informative, specific but most of all experiential. Use words carefully to create a mental picture of what it would be like to stay in that apartment. An actual picture of the room, as long as it is favourable, goes a long way too.

5. **Corporate Speak** - Ensure you have a "Public Corporate Rate" among your offerings. Many Travel Agencies or Web Search portals look specifically for "corporate" rate codes when searching for their business clients. If you do not have one (even if it is simply the same as your Rack Rate or Best Available Rate) then you will not be included in these searches and could miss out on valuable business.

Distribution

In this section, I am going to talk about how to distribute your apartments on the OTAs effectively. I will also give you a list of all the relevant short term bookings OTAs.

An online travel agency, or OTA, is a website or online service, which sells travel related products to customers. These products may include hotels, flights, travel packages, activities and car rentals. Crucially, OTAs are third parties, reselling these services on behalf of other companies, including those in the hotel industry.

Typically, an OTA will offer many of the benefits of using an offline travel agency, with added convenience and more of a self-service approach. They will also include a built-in booking system, allowing for instant bookings.

The Most Important Online Distribution Channel

Although online travel agencies can play a vital role in terms of distribution, allowing those within the hotel industry to reach a wider audience, it is important to understand that your own website should always be the number one priority. After all, bookings made through your website do not require you to pay commission to a third party, which is important for revenue management, as it maximises the amount of money you actually receive.

Online travel agents are increasingly important for serviced apartments, because they serve as both a marketing and a distribution channel. A growing number of potential guests now turn to OTAs to search for their accommodation, because they function as a kind of' one *stop shop',* allowing them to easily search for apartments, hotels, read reviews, and compare prices.

In addition, apartments that are listed on online travel agent websites can also benefit from what is sometimes referred to as the *'billboard effect'.* This refers to the fact that OTAs can provide a form of advertising, making their users aware of the serviced apartment business on their platform. After gaining this awareness, users may then decide to research a provider and perhaps even go on to make a direct booking through the providers website. This is something that has happened to me many many times when I've listed on the OTAs. It's also why I keep preaching about the importance of having an online presence away from the OTAs. Research has showed that 40% of all OTA users do a Google search of the accommodation they are thinking of booking after finding it on an OTA.

How Does Commission Work With Online Travel Agents?

Effectively, online travel agents make bookings on behalf of their users, and they make money by charging a commission fee to suppliers. The precise fee can vary significantly from service to service, but is generally a percentage of the amount paid by the customer.

In most cases, the commission fee is paid either after the customer has made their final payment, or after the travel itself has been completed. The commission fee varies per online travel agent. For example the commission of Booking.com could be somewhere between 10 and 18%, whereas Expedia charges between 18 and between 25%. Higher fees can be charged in exchange for a higher ranking within search results. This is the trade-off for those in the hotel industry, because an OTA can help them to sell rooms, but it is also likely to be one of their most expensive distribution channels.

12 Online Travel Agents Your Brand Should Be Working With

There are a wide range of online travel agencies on the market and it is an industry that is growing all the time, especially as new technology emerges. Below you will find 12 of the most significant OTAs that serviced accommodation operators can consider to increase there visibility and bookings..

Booking.com

Booking.com is owned by the same company as Priceline, and is one of the oldest online travel agents, having been originally founded in 1996. The business has its headquarters in Amsterdam, in the Netherlands, and the website has listings which cover close to 200 different countries around the world. Like many OTAs on the market, Booking.com offers users the ability to book hotels, motels, holiday homes and other similar accommodation types, while also functioning as a travel fare aggregation service.

Expedia.com is a travel booking service and the main OTA operated by the Expedia Group, which also owns a number of subsidiaries. It is based in Bellevue, Washington, in the United States and was founded in 2001. It is one of the highest grossing travel companies in the world and has localised sites in 40 countries. Customers can book hotels, holiday homes, B&Bs, flights, rental cars, activities and other travel services. In terms of marketing, it places an emphasis on cheap and affordable accommodation.

Hotels.com is a service which allows users to book hotels, B&B accommodation and condos online. It is based in Dallas, Texas, in the United States and is owned by the Expedia Group. The platform operates on an international scale and a huge part of its business model is based on repeat business. Indeed, a major component of the company's offering is the *Hotels.com Rewards'* scheme, where users can claim a price reduction after every 10 overnight stays that are booked through the service. Hotels.com is part of The Expedia Group.

Since Hotels.com is part of the Expedia Group, your apartment will visible on Hotels.com when listed to Expedia.

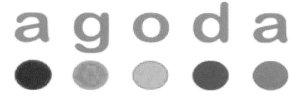

Agoda.com is a global accommodation booking service, which is based in Singapore. Like several other OTAs on this list, it forms part of Booking Holdings; the parent company behind Booking.com. The Agoda network provides users with a choice of over one million hotels or holiday homes, with a strong focus on the Asian market, although it is increasingly targeting Europe and the Americas too. In terms of its approach to marketing, the company places a strong emphasis on providing customers with cheap or discount accommodation.

As previously stated, Priceline.com is owned by Booking Holdings, the same company that operates Booking.com. However, the Priceline.com company has its headquarters in Norwalk, Connecticut, in the United States. The main difference between Priceline.com and Booking.com is that Priceline.com focuses even more heavily on the discount travel market. To achieve this, it offers a 'Name Your Own Price' model, where customers are able to set their ideal price, location and hotel star level, and the service will then find a suitable option.

Since Piceline.com partnered up with Agoda.com, your apartment will visible on Priceline.com when listed to Agoda.com

HRS.com is an online travel agent website, which is based in Cologne, Germany, with major offices in London, Paris and New York. It began life as an offline travel agency, and the company itself was founded back in 1972. While the HRS.com service provides hotel bookings for both private travellers and business travellers, it places a clear focus on the latter group, promoting a special 30 percent discount, or 'business rate'. It can, therefore, be an excellent choice for apartments which are prioritising business customers too.

Airbnb is an online hospitality marketplace, which allows members to offer lodgings or to book overnight stays. Its offerings primarily consist of home stays, although the brand has branched out and now lists hotels too. However, Airbnb tends to be quite strict about the hotels it will allow to be listed on its platform, as they must meet certain criteria. Typically, a hotel will need to prove that it has unique design characteristics, that its rooms have a clear local influence, and that guests have access to shared common spaces. For that reason there's not that much competition from hotels so it makes it a viable platform to list your apartment.

Orbitz. com is an online travel metasearch engine and OTA, which serves as a subsidiary of the Expedia Group. Although it is primarily geared towards the American market, it provides a range of international travel options. Aside from offering hotel bookings, it also caters for flights, car rentals, cruises and package deals. The service was acquired by the Expedia Group in 2015, with several sources stating that it would help them to compete with the Priceline.com component of Booking Holdings' business model.

LateRooms.com

Since Orbitz.com is part of the Expedia Group, your apartment will visible on Orbitz.com when listed to Expedia.

LateRooms.com is a dedicated hotel reservation platform, which is based in Manchester, in the United Kingdom. The company was founded in 1999, but did not offer online hotel bookings until 2002. As a platform, LateRooms.com places a clear emphasis on attracting customers looking for last minute deals on overnight stays, including bookings for the very same day. In many cases, these late deals are sold at a discount. As a result, it can be a solid option for serviced apartments that are prone to having spare inventory that they need to fill during the week.

Based in Shanghai, China, Trip.com is the largest online travel agency in the country. It primarily targets the Chinese market, including both domestic and international travellers, and the vast majority of its sales come from people living in the cities of Shanghai, Beijing, Shenzhen, and Guangzhou. Trip also has a strategic partnership in place with Booking.com, which allows the Chinese company to access Booking.com's global portfolio, and allows Booking.com to gain greater access to the Chinese market.

The Travelocity.com brand was founded in 1996, making it one of the older active OTAs on the market, and it too is now owned by the Expedia Group. The company has its headquarters in Dallas, Texas, in the United States. In terms of how it differentiates itself from its parent brand, Travelocity places an increased focus on package deals and on providing positive travel experiences. One of its unique features is a *'Travel for Good'* scheme, where customers are rewarded if they participate in volunteering opportunities while on their travels.

Since Travelocity.com is part of the Expedia Group, your apartment will visible on Travelocity.com when listed to Expedia.

How to Distribute Your Serviced Apartment Inventory With All Online Distribution Agencies?

For serviced apartments that opt to use online travel agencies, one of the major challenges involves distributing an apartment's inventory to as many online platforms as possible. The best solution to this problem is to use a distribution channel management solution, which allows the various distribution channels to be managed from a single place. I have a list of recommended channel managers at the end of this book.

Tips to Increase Your Apartment Bookings Through Online Travel Agents

Online travel agents, or OTAs, are a vital part of the

marketing mix and also function as a major distribution channel. Of course, with these OTAs taking a commission for bookings made through their platforms, it is crucial that you optimise your apartments' listings and maximise the value these services provide.

While OTAs are a key distribution channel in the modern age, they do not guarantee success on their own and it is important to adopt some best practices. Below, you will find 10 tips to help you increase apartment bookings.

1. Find the Right OTA Mix

A vital first step is to make sure you find the right OTA mix, so that you are reaching your target audiences. This means taking the time to research different OTAs and then partnering with the right ones. It also means managing distribution, so that you optimise both revenue and profit for your business.

2. Use a Distribution Channel Manager

A channel manager is an application which enables you to manage your various distribution channels from a central point. Using one can help you to avoid situations where you need to access each OTA individually, on by one, in order to make adjustments to things like room rates or room availability.

This can help to facilitate a far more dynamic pricing strategy, where you can make adjustments to prices on a single OTA, or all OTAs at the same time, depending on what you are trying to achieve. The ability to do this quickly and effortlessly, in real-time, makes it far easier to respond to spikes or dips in demand for your apartments.

3. Build a Relationship with Market Managers

While online travel agents offer a lot of self-service options for customers, those in the hotel industry need to recognise the human element of working with an OTA and a major example of this involves developing a good relationship with market managers. Doing so may require you to invite market managers to your business, or go to lunch with them.

In return, market managers will be more willing to work with you, helping you to devise promotional strategies and spot trends related to your serviced apartment, which can help you to understand where you are going right and where you are going wrong. A market manager has the power to drive demand to your serviced apartment, so make it worth their while to do so. When I operated in London, I had 30 apartments I was operating in different boroughs. One of the market managers from booking.com (Natalia Ros) actually reached out and came to our office during her lunch break so she can get to know us a bit better. I spent about two hours with her in Canary Wharf and those two hours were very insightful. Her influence and knowledge just made it a more pleasant experience dealing with booking.com in terms of scaling up and knowing which areas have high demand.

4. Use Amazing Photographs

When it comes to selling your apartment to potential customers, a picture is worth a thousand words. High-quality photographs can help you to make a great first impression and provide you with a chance to clearly highlight what your business has to offer. Yet, there are a few best practices to keep in mind when creating apartment images.

Use the best possible equipment and identify the best parts of your apartment. Try to take photos that show people enjoying your apartments, rather than showcasing empty rooms, and take the time to arrange things the way you want them. If you are taking photos outside, time it to highlight either excellent weather, or atmospheric night time views.

5. Stand Out With Your Description

While using an OTA, customers are likely to look at more than one apartment provider and this means you need to make yours stand out. Aside from promoting its qualities using photos, your description plays a key role. You need to clearly describe the type of apartment you operate and what it has to offer, but you should also try to be creative.

Think about the type of customer(s) you are targeting and speak to them. If you are targeting families, make sure your description says you are *"family-oriented"*. Remember, you do not need to stick to describing the apartment alone. Talk about the nearby attractions and promote the fact that your apartment offers easy access to them.

6. Know Your Competition

The serviced apartment industry is now extremely

competitive and your apartment and your main rivals are likely to be vying for the same customers on the same OTAs. For this reason, it is important to take the time to get to know your competition, understand what they have to offer customers.

This can involve independent research, checking online feedback and monitoring prices. You want to be sure that you are not either over-pricing or under-pricing your apartments, based on what similar apartments are charging. Moreover, if you can start to identify problems with rival apartments, you can start to appeal to the people they are letting down.

7. The Right Price for The Right Moment

Adopting the right pricing strategy is crucial for increasing bookings through OTAs, and it is important that you charge the right price for the right moment. Two of the main pricing strategies involve setting your prices based on demand, and maintaining price parity across all distribution channels.

The former strategy involves forecasting demand, based on past data, current bookings and wider industry trends. At times of higher demand, you can charge more, while lowering prices when demand is low can help to fill your apartment. Price parity (same rates for the same room on all the distribution channels, including your own website) is essential for being accepted onto some OTA platforms, but you do need to be careful when setting your standardised rate, as different OTAs will charge you different commission for the same room rates.

8. Manage Guest Reviews

A large number of customers read online reviews before making a booking, so it is essential that you take the time to manage your guest reviews. There are a number of ways to achieve this, starting from delivering an excellent customer experience, encouraging your guests to leave reviews, and taking the time to respond to feedback.

Try to identify any common complaints quickly and work to resolve the issues. Make sure you keep all information about your apartment up-to-date, so people do not have false expectations, and try not to get unnecessarily defensive. It is better to admit your mistakes and strive to improve than it is to blame the customer or deny the problem exists.

9. Make Use of OTA Promotion Opportunities

One of the ways those in the serviced apartment industry can take full advantage of what online travel agents have to offer is by capitalising on some of the special offers that are available. This can be especially important during periods of low demand, where making sure apartments are occupied becomes the main priority.

Examples of some of the promotional opportunities available include paying for higher placement on OTA search engines, or running ad campaigns to target specific demographics at specific times. You may also be able to pay higher commission in exchange for greater exposure, or join special deal promotions offered by some OTAs.

10. Continually Review Your OTA Results

Finally, even when following all of the tips provided, it is unlikely you will create the perfect OTA strategy at the first time of asking. It is, therefore, imperative to continually review your results, so that you have a clear idea of how your apartment is performing, what is going right, and where there is room for improvement.

Take the time to monitor results and make adjustments to pricing when necessary. Pay attention to which online travel agents are working well for you and which ones are failing to generate the right return on investment. Keep track of key metrics and make sure you discuss new or alternative opportunities with the various market managers.

Platforms for medium to long stay bookings

In this section I am going to give you a list of platform that specialise in medium to long term bookings. I think it's very important to have a good mix in distributing your apartments, however, relevancy is very important. There is no point in listing your apartment on a platform that cater for party people when you want to avoid them.

hometogo

HomeToGo is an independent metasearch engine for vacation rentals that compares more than 15,565,757 worldwide offers from over 300 listing websites. It's a popular platform in Europe so you'd get a lot of guests relocating from Spain or Germany coming from there.

With properties in over 22,600 cities & 131 countries, BridgeStreet is the travel technology leader for extended stays. This platform is popular with business travelers from all over the world. You need a min of 5 properties to list with them.

HouseStay.com offers a curated selection of fully furnished apartments & homes available for 30+ night stays. You need a minimum of 5 properties to list with these guys.

Homelike

A marketplace for long-term business apartments that offers one of the largest selections of furnished apartments with a portfolio of 100 cities in Europe. You also need a min of 5 properties to list with this platform.

AltoVita, the platform for extended stays and repeat guests. Based in the UK with an average night of 40 nights being booked on their platform, this platform makes it a very relevant distribution option. You need a minimum of 5 properties to list with them.

I hope you have found value in this section. Building a professional short rental business is elaborate and learning how to effectively distribute your apartment rentals online is arguably the first and most important step to success. By now you're surely quite familiar with the big OTA's and understand that listing on these sites is essential to your business success. However, when it comes to advertising on niche sites, I discovered that not many property managers/ operators are including them in their marketing strategies. As of 2020, it is essential for property managers to incorporate niche sites as diversifying the marketing mix will allow businesses to tap into new clients and markets, and will minimise the risks of algorithm changes, or worse OTA bankruptcy. Diverting some focus to niche markets has the potential to significantly increase marketing ROI as strategies become both cheaper and more effective with less competition.

In the next chapter and sub chapters I will be taking you through the Direct mail and Online marketing strategies I use today. These tactics have enabled me to successfully manage 25+ apartments without the need for OTAs like booking.com

Chapter 6

Direct Marketing Strategies and Application

Objective: To learn how to use direct marketing strategies to attract and convert direct bookings from corporate clients and business clients.

Why don't we get the results we want from other people? Husbands and wives routinely complain about their spouses expecting them to be mind readers. Managers bemoan employees' failures to perform as expected, often saying, " But I told him once." Most managers idea about training omit a feedback loop to ascertain comprehension and acceptance, and ignore the need for perpetual reinforcement. Everywhere you look in human-to-human communication, there is disappointment. This certainly exists for marketers too, although many business owners don't think they should be able to outright control the behaviour of their customers to the extent they should be able to employees, vendors, or family members. In marketing and sales, control is exactly what we need. Ultimately, all this Is much about simple clarity. Do people really, clearly know what's expected of them? Or are you taking too much for granted, chalking things up as too obvious to bother clarifying?

So with that in mind, I have some rules for you to follow. From now on, every advert you run, every leaflet or booklet you you mail or distribute, every website you put up, every/ anything you do to advertise or market your business MUST adhere to these rules:

Rule 1. You must always present an offer

Rule 2. You will give them a reason to respond immediately

Rule 3. Your copy will give clear instructions

Rule 4. You shall track, measure and be accountable

Rule 5. You must follow-up

Rule 6. Your copy will be strong

Rule 7. Results will rule!. Period.

Rule 8. You will need to be tough minded and put your business on a direct marketing diet!

By now you might be asking yourself; what is direct marketing and why is it different to any other kind of marketing?

Well, to put it simply, **direct marketing** is designed to provoke an **IMMEDIATE** response from a customer or a specific group of people, through clear CTAs (calls to action) and other techniques, in order to generate reactions and feedback while encouraging decision-making. The biggest advantage to this type of marketing is that it's cheap as you are targeting a subset group of people, and that it's also trackable and measurable, meaning you can scale it at will.

Indirect marketing is to focus on platforms where there they have no direct communication with customers. This strategy is useful for keeping customers and increasing their loyalty, as well as expanding the business and brand. One of the common ways companies market indirectly is by using public relations to present a consistent image. The biggest problem with this type of marketing for small operators like us is that it's expensive because you're marketing indirectly to just anyone, and it's not trackable, therefore not measurable; how can you scale what you can't measure?

Now that you know what direct marketing is, here is what your outbound marketing funnel needs to look like:

Tools/ assets needed:

- An email list of corporate clients and businesses in your chosen location.

- A CRM to prospect and manage communication with your email list.

- A website with details of your brand and your apartments

- A professional telephone number (0800 or geographical)

- A professional email address (no gmail or hotmail)

- Your company brochure

Email List for prospecting

When you are looking for new business, you have to prospect. In these days, one of the best ways to prospect is by email.

The first thing you want to do is to open an account with a CRM provider. CRM means customer relationship management. It will help you keep track of all the emails going in and out of your business. Imagine trying to send 1000 emails to different people using gmail? It's virtually impossible. Besides, if you are going to buy an email list, conventional newsletter clients like Mailchimp won't allow you to send emails to people who haven't given you specific permission to write to them. I now use Zendesk Sell in my company but feel free to shop around and see what works for you.

After opening an account with a CRM of your choice, your next step will be to set it up by adding your company email address, logo, signature, phone number and inviting any other team members in your company who will be working with you on prospecting. After that, you will need to upload a .csv file of your email list.

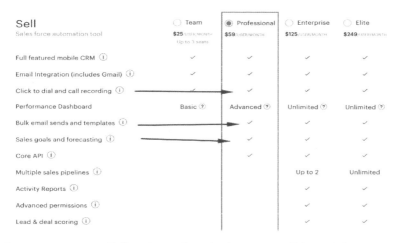

Sell	Team	Professional	Enterprise	Elite
Sales force automation tool	$25 USER/MONTH Up to 3 seats	$59 USER/MONTH	$125 USER/MONTH	$249 USER/MONTH
Full featured mobile CRM	✓	✓	✓	✓
Email Integration (includes Gmail)	✓	✓	✓	✓
Click to dial and call recording	✓	✓	✓	✓
Performance Dashboard	Basic	Advanced	Unlimited	Unlimited
Bulk email sends and templates		✓	✓	✓
Sales goals and forecasting		✓	✓	✓
Core API		✓	✓	✓
Multiple sales pipelines			Up to 2	Unlimited
Activity Reports			✓	✓
Advanced permissions			✓	✓
Lead & deal scoring			✓	✓

When your email list is uploaded, you will be able to send bulk emails to all the prospects in one go. However, before you send any email, you need to adhere to GDPR regulations. And that rule specifies that, you are in breach of GDPR if you send email communication for the means of selling if you haven't got their permission or have a legitimate interest in doing so. So how do we gain legitimate interest? By physically writing to them first! Direct mail is not bound by GDPR regulations so you can essentially 'cold write' to anyone you want, provided you give them an **opportunity to opt out.**

As serviced accommodation providers, we want the opportunity to show your prospects what you have to offer and how it benefits the client. To do that we design a simple, but effective piece of direct marketing brochure. Please see an example below from one of our locations:

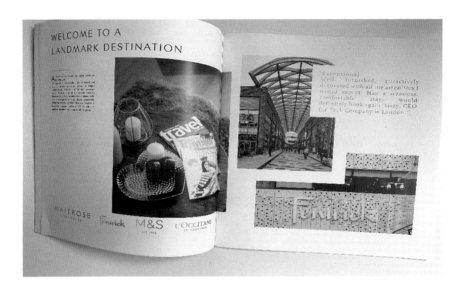

THE WELCOME APARTMENTS

WELCOME APARTMENTS LOVE CORPORATES & SMALL BUSINESS TRAVELLERS

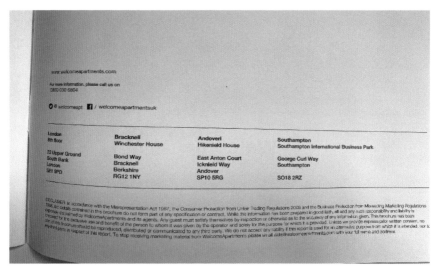

We made this brochure in an online app called Canva It cost us £0 to make this brochure. The printers we use are called InstantPrint.co.uk.

Here is the spec of the booklet shown above:

A4 210mm x 297mm Stapled Booklets

A4 210mm x 297mm, Double Sided, Value Silk 150gsm , Saddle Stitched, 24pp, No Lamination

Cost £750.00 for 1,000

Now that you have the CRM and brochures ready, it's time to find the email addresses and physical mailing addresses for the companies you're going to be sending these marketing pieces to.

Getting GDPR compliant email lists of corporate companies

There are two options for this; you either buy them from a data company like Data House UK or you can build one yourself with Experian B2B Prospecting tool. If you decide to use a data company, all you have to do is call them and give them your requirements.

Requirements for one of the locations example:

Search Criteria	Standard Details per Record	Additional Details per Record	Usage
Email Type	• Contact Name	• Email Address	• Multiple Usage
Admin Emails:	• Salutation	• Safe To Email	
No Admin emails	• First Name	• Turnover	**Last Modified By**
AND	• Surname	• SIC 2007	emilia day
Contact Type	• Company Name	• SIC 1992	
Job Function:			
Senior Decision Maker, Director,			
Director (Non-Executive),			
Finance, General Manager, HR,			
HR / Personnel, Logistics,			
Management, Manager /			
Executive, Managing Director,			
Office Management, Operations,			
Personal Assistant, Project			
Management			
AND			
Business Size			
Turnover:			
3 : 90k to <400k, 4 : 400k to			
<1m, 5 : 1m to <2.5m, 6 : 2.5m to			
<5m, 7 : 5m to <10m, 8 : 10m to			
<40m, 9 : 40m+			
AND			

Note: *ensure you have a mailing address, email address as well as phone number for all or most of your contacts. If you're unable to have all the list usage requirements, the minimum should be email address and mailing address.*

Sending the brochures

When you've received your brochures from the printers, you need to check that they have printed as expected because the next step will be to send them to your prospects. For this part, I recommend to use UKmail or Royal Mail Door to Door Marketing service. Prices vary depending on weight and amount of materials to be sent so you need to call them and get a quote. There are other companies that offer a leaflet/ marketing drop service. Do a Google search and get quotes from at least 3 suppliers. Once you've found a suitable company to do the drop, they will usually arrange to come to you and pick up the materials, they will pack them and send them out on a specific date or timescale that's agreeable to you. Just make sure they have the ability to tell you when all the brochures have been delivered, because after that you will be able to send an email to the prospects roughly a week after confirmed delivery. We need to wait at least 7 days because if your prospects want to opt out, 7 days is ample time for them to do that. When you are ready to send the bulk email, your first email has to be relevant and get the attention of the recipient. Here's a template of the first contact email.

SUBJECT: {First name}, did you get the brochure?

Hi {First name}

Hope you are well. I'm writing to you today because I am really keen to find out how I can save your company at least X% on accommodation costs for your employees. I sent you a brochure last week with details of our accommodation and wondered if you're free for a quick chat in the next few days? In fact, I am going to be in {TOWN} next week meeting with XXX Ltd, so if this is something you're interested in finding out more about then feel free to let me know what your usual accommodation requirements are so I can put together a meaningful proposal for you. Last year we saved XXX Ltd over £40,000 in accommodation costs so I'm sure we can help you meet your travel budget goals as well.

If this is not your department, I would appreciate it if you could point me in the right direction.

I won't take up much more of your time, I look forward to hearing from you.

Regards

Jane Doe

Key Account Manager

0208 123 456

PS- book with us in the next 30 days and get 40% off your reservation.

As you can see, the email template is simple, straight to the point, has an offer, encourages the recipient to reply straight away, and clearly shows why you might be able to benefit them. Decision makers are very busy people and the last thing they want is to read 'waffle' from a stranger. And I promise, if they are not interested, you will get a polite email back saying so.

The key thing to remember here is the objective of your email prospecting is to get on the phone with the client or to meet up in person at their office or at your apartments so you can have a meaningful discussion about how you can work together. The hard sell way of selling doesn't work anymore, in fact it's so dated you'd probably be reported for spam if you tried it today. In my experience, cold calling a business and not knowing who to ask for is just time wasting. You need to be able to have genuine rapport with the prospect if you want to be in with a chance of setting up a meeting in person or over the phone.

Another important thing to remember is that we are small operators, so if you haven't got enough inventory , it could cause problems with business clients. That's why I advise all my students to have a partnership/ relationship with other providers in the building. This is because if you manage to get 5 clients who want to book with you regularly, they are going to have different dates of arrival which will overlap, especially if you have less than 10 units. The best way to avoid disappointment and potentially lose a client is to partner up with a reputable provider and charge them commission. The client doesn't need to know that the apartment you've booked them in doesn't belong to you, as long as they get the same service and amenities found in your own apartments.

So, that is the process of prospecting business and corporate clients. It's something you should do consistently until you have enough clients booking with you.

Tips for making your email marketing a success

Email marketing outperforms all online marketing strategies, including SEO, PPC, and content marketing like blogging and PR!

An **email marketing strategy** is an important part of any marketing strategy. Email is the most cost-effective way to promote your products, communicate with your guests and reach your business goals.

And on average, for every £1 you spend on email marketing, you can expect a return of £51 (up from £39 last year)!

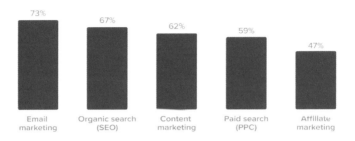

Not bad, right?

Here, I will share the best email marketing strategies you can use to achieve extraordinary results through email marketing using your CRM or newsletter client like Mailchimp, Aweber, Constant Contact etc

5 strategies for better email marketing campaigns

When you follow these email marketing strategies, email will become your most important channel too!

Let's get started.

1: Personalise your messages

When I say personalised email marketing, I don't mean that you send an individual email to every single subscriber. Personalisation means that you use customer data to create a personalised message.

A great example of a company that does personalisation

well is **Booking.com**.

All of Booking.com's emails are personalised.

It's not "Dear valued customer", but "Dear Steven".

It's not, "You might like these... (randomly generated)", but "You might like these (based on my browsing history)".

To Booking.com, email marketing is not just another marketing channel. It's key to of the overall customer experience.

Another example is Jeff Bezos, Amazon's CEO is an email mastermind. Jeff Bezos understands the value of emails and has been known to read through customer complaints. It's also why more than 35% of all product sales come from recommendations (both via email and on screen).

And it's not just Amazon that have seen these kinds of results through personalisation.

A study by Experian found that personalized emails deliver 6x higher transaction rates!

Let's break this down into numbers we can all understand:

The most recent research found that email marketing generates £0.08 in revenue per email.

That may not sound like much...

But if you send out an email campaign to 500,000 subscribers, **you can generate up to £40,000 in revenue.**

That's a lot of additional revenue!

But, if you use personalisation in your emails, you can

expect a lot more!

According to brand new research by LiveClicker,

Personalisation can generate £20 in ROI for every £1 invested.

How's that for a revenue opportunity?

The best part is this:

70% of brands **do not use personalisation** within their email marketing strategy.

This means that by personalising your emails, you stand out against the competition.

The simplest form of personalisation is to address the reader by name. Most email service providers (ESP) offer this within their functionality and this tactic alone will improve your campaign performance.

For example, email subject lines that are personalized with a recipient's first name can increase open rates by 16% higher open rates.

Considering that 47% of all emails are opened because of subject line alone, that's a sure fire way to get more eyeballs on your email.

Outside of using the customer's name, here are a few more tips to help you get started with personalisation:

- **Ask for the right information upfront:** Great personalisation starts way before you hit the 'send ' button. It all starts with your sign up form. Without data such as name, company and location, you will be very limited with your personalised communication. Remember to only ask for the information you need, rather than the information you want. This is one of the ways that GDPR has impacted marketing teams.

- **Use a real reply-to email address:** When you use donotreply@example.com, it takes away the authenticity from the messaging. You want your readers to engage and respond to your campaigns. Use a real reply address will improve credibility and appear more personal.

- **Use your real email signature:** Just like using a real reply-to email address, you want to use real contact information within the email and the best way to do that is to include your contact details in the email signature. Giving your readers the opportunity to contact you or connect with you online is a great way to be personal and build a relationship with them.

2: Segment your subscribers

According to email marketers, segmentation is second on the top initiatives list this year.

Do you know why it is so high?

It's because when you segment your database, your email campaigns become much more targeted to your audience.

Let's take a look at an example:

You're hosting a property networking event for property

investors located within a 20 mile radius.

How can you expect to get the best turn out for your event?

The answer is **segmentation.**

The best way to get small business owners to turn up to your event would be to create a segment of people who list themselves as a property investor that lives within 20 miles of your event and then send them an invite by email. The segmentation part is simple and can easily be done through CRM software.

Compare this to sending one email to your entire database, with subscribers spread across the country (or continent).

How annoying is it to receive an email that invites you to an event that is located on other side of the world?

It's very annoying!

Another example is when you are up and running and guests are checking in, they are going to be coming from different parts of the country. So when you have an offer promote, you want to be able to segment the email by adding the date or month that they stayed. You email could look like this:

"Dear John,

Thank you for staying with us on {DATE OF ARRIVAL}

Just to let you know that we currently have a special offer for our {CITY} location, if you book with us again this year, you are qualified to get 25% off your reservation. This offer is valid for the next 7 days only so let us know as soon as possible if you'd like to reserve your apartment and save!

Regards

Jane Doe"

As you can see the email above is highly personalised, it's not an email that looks like it's been sent to hundreds of other people (even though it has), but that's the beauty of personalisation. It makes the guest/ customer feel important.

Before you start segmenting your database, let's take a look at how valuable it can be.

A study by HubSpot found that all email marketing KPIs perform better when you segment your email list.

If you segment your lists, you get better open rates, revenue, leads, transactions and more customers.

Another benefit is that segmentation goes hand in hand with GDPR and email marketing.

But, does it really work?

Yes!

Here's an example from my own email marketing campaigns:

I recently sent out two email marketing campaigns. Both campaigns had the same subject line and the same content.

The first campaign was sent to our non-segmented email list, while the second was sent to our segmented list (segmented by pages visited on our website).

The first non-segmented email earned an impressive 42 % open rate and a 4.5% click-through rate.

However, the segmented email campaign earned **a 94% open rate and a 38% click-through rate!**

I'd say it's pretty valuable, wouldn't you?

And that's why so many serviced accommodation operators 'are segmenting their emails, right?

Wrong.

Because 9 out of 10 serviced accommodation brands 'do not segment their database.

So, here are a few examples for you to get started with segmentation:

- **Segment by date of arrival:** when you address a previous guest's date of arrival it shows that you know and care about the guest.

- **Segment by company size**: Also known as account-based marketing, segmenting email campaigns by company size or annual revenue is a great way to increase response rates. A small business that employs 5 people is not likely ready for a paid loyalty card, whereas a business that employs 750 people might be a better fit.

- **Segment by location stayed**: segmenting guests by the location or apartment they stayed brings you to top of mind straight away. I recently received an email from booking.com saying " we know you stayed in Southampton recently, we thought you might be interested in these vacation rentals nearby" These vacation rentals where in Portsmouth, which was quite handy because I had been planning a trip to the Gunwharf Quays outlet with my children for later that month so it made it easy for me to remember to look at the options available. When the time came, I didn't book with booking.com as I like to book direct with the provider, however they served as a 'billboard' for the provider which benefited them.

3. Send mobile friendly emails

In 2012, 27% of all marketing emails were opened on a mobile device.

By 2014, that number jumped up to 42%.

Now, it's as high as 61%!

These are huge numbers!

And what do you do as soon as you wake up in the morning?

If you're like me, I'm guessing you have your phone next to your bed and the first thing you do each morning is check your phone for calls, messages and yes, you guessed it, emails...

Don't worry, you're not the only one. 62% of us do this.

When you send an email to a subscriber who reads their emails on their mobile device, but the email is not optimised for that device, what do you think they do with?

Mostly, they will unsubscribe or delete it.

So why is it that almost half of all emails are still not mobile friendly?

Worse still, KissMetrics's email marketing research found that 20% of email campaigns are not optimised for mobile.

Yet on the opposite end of the scale, and when email campaigns are optimised for mobile, they generate a lot of revenue!

The average revenue per mobile email is £0.40, which is more than 4x that of a desktop email click, according to Yesmail.

Revenue per email on mobile devices is 4X higher than desktop

And 55% of smartphone users have made at least one purchase after receiving a mobile promotional email.

Furthermore, a study by Flexmail found that 36% of B2B companies that have optimised their email campaigns for mobile devices saw an overall improvement to their email performance.

So, how do you optimise your campaigns for mobile devices?

Don't worry, here are some tips on how to do that.

- **Implement responsive email design (RED):** Creating a responsive email design means that the user experience is optimised regardless of the device or screen they use. Most email service providers (ESP) offer this solution within their email functionality.

- **Keep the subject line and pre-header short**: The subject line is crucial. Keep it short so the reader knows exactly what the email topic is about. And the pre-header text (also known as snippet text), don't let it go to waste by using "To view this email in your browser…". Instead, summarise the email or include a call to action (i.e., Use "FREENIGHT" to get a free night if they stay for three).

- **Make the CTA big and obvious**: Mobile device vary in size. While a text link may work on a tablet or larger screen, you might be alienating your readers who have a smaller screen (or bigger hands!) if your call to action is too small. Make the call to action, big, bold and simple to click.

4. Test copy, design and buttons

Whether you test your home page, landing pages or email templates, testing provides us with data to make practical decisions that will improve our marketing performance.

And email marketing is no different.

Sure, you've probably tested subject lines before – who hasn't?

Even the former President of the United States has A/B tested his email subject lines….

Think I'm joking?

According to Bloomberg, email marketing played a huge part in the success of Obama's 2012 Presidential campaign.

By sending several variations made to the subject line to a small sample of subscribers, they were able to calculate the amount in donations they could expect to receive based on the results.

The sample size revealed that the poorest performing subject line ("The one thing the polls got right.."), when sent to the entire database, would generate $403,603 in donations.

The best performing subject line ("I will be outspent") was expected to generate $2,540,866 in donations.

That's a huge difference!

In fact, the best performing subject line outperformed expectations and generated a total of $2,673,278.

That's an additional $2.2 million in donations raised due to a change in the emails subject line!

President Barack Obama raised an additional $2 million in donations by split testing his email subject line

But it's not only subject lines you can test through email marketing.

You can also test:

- **From address:** The name that appears in the "from" field has a huge impact on whether the reader opens your email. In fact, the sender name is the main reason why people open your email. Test your from address by sending your campaigns from a person's name, person + company or from your CEO.

- **Plain text vs HTML campaigns:** Like most

companies', I'm sure you are already sending a plain text version of your email. However, have you thought of testing an email campaign that is plain text only? And when you add an element of personalisation, plain text emails appear to be written just for the reader.

- **Long vs short emails**: You can keep your emails short and sweet or, you can create long detailed emails. Long form emails can include more detailed copy whereas shorter emails will send the reader directly to a targeted landing page. The best way to see what works best? Test it.

5. Automate email campaigns when possible

Trigger-based emails are emails that are sent out automatically based on user behavior.

The most common forms of trigger emails are 'welcome ' emails, 'thank you 'emails and 'transactional 'emails, such as booking confirmation email and email receipts.

The data behind trigger emails shows us that trigger emails perform much better than traditional email.

For example, Epsilon found that:

- Open rates for trigger emails are as high as 49% (95% higher than traditional email open rates)

- The average click-through rate (CTR) for trigger emails is more than double the rate compared to traditional email click-through rates

- The best converting websites in the world, sites that

convert as much as 40% of their traffic, use trigger emails.

And not only that, Forrester research found that trigger-based email marketing campaigns can **generate 4x more revenue and 18x greater profits!**

Does this sound too good to be true?

Well, it's not. I've tested it. And it works!

My triggered emails generated 5x higher open rates and 15x higher click-through rates.

Today, only 25% of hospitality business owners currently use triggered emails and they make up a low percentage of overall email volume, at around 2.6%. However, they can be responsible for as **much as 20% of your email marketing revenue!**

Triggered emails perform really well because they hit the email marketing sweet spot.

What does the email marketing sweet spot look like, you ask?

It looks like this:

And the reason why they perform so well is because of **context.**

Consider the following scenario;

You visit a website, browse the product line and add items to your shopping cart but, you begin to have doubts and decide to leave before completing a purchase.

Sound familiar?

This happens to every single eCommerce store, every

single day.

But what if, one hour later, you receive an email that includes the exact product you were shopping for?

And what if this email included not only a quick-link back to your shopping cart but, a free shipping code or 10% discount?

You're now more likely to complete your purchase, aren't you?

That's the power of trigger emails.

But setting up triggered emails is expensive and complex, isn't it?

It doesn't have to be. You can start by using auto-responders in your customer service software to replicate the automation aspect. That's what I do for all of my existing triggered emails and I'm happy with it.

Here are some examples of trigger mails you can send;

- **Activation:** A new guest books one of your apartments. You can send them an email that shows them how to pick up the keys and check in.

- **Surprise:** Guest loyalty is the key to success. And you can reward your loyal guests by giving them something for free every now and then. Create a "surprise" email that sends an automated email to your best guests that offers a free stay if they reserve for X amount of nights. It's a small cost for your business but, the reward is huge!

Conclusion

Email marketing continues to deliver results.

But email marketing has evolved. It's no longer as simple as sending the same email to all.

It's time to start or update your email marketing strategy.

Now, you need to send targeted messages. Messages that are personalised, and optimised for multiple devices.

You also need test new elements. Trends change quickly, and what worked 12 months ago may not be successful today. Be open to testing. And when you understand what works, find ways to automate it through triggered emails.

If you implement these new changes into your email marketing strategy your guests will be more responsive, your campaign performance will improve and your business will continue grow.

Channels to be discovered on for direct bookings:

In this section, I am going to over all the relevant platforms guests use to be inspired, do research, and ultimately book accommodation.

Google Adwords

Google AdWords is a powerful tool, reaching up to 90% of users worldwide. It's the power behind, of course, the ads you see when you search on Google, but also behind countless image ads on thousands of sites across the web. Google AdWords is a valuable resource, and it's one that most modern hotels rely on as a major part of their marketing strategy.

That said, AdWords 'interface can easily confuse inexperienced users. The multitude of options for campaigns and campaign settings makes it almost impossible to choose the right ones, unless you're an expert.

To make life a little simpler, I have identified **the** 5 most important types of campaigns for the serviced apartment industry. In this section, I'll be talking about how to run them, which metrics to watch out for, and why they work so well for serviced apartments.

Let's get started.

THE SEARCH NETWORK

The Search Network is where I recommend all hotels start. Users on the Google search platform are actively looking for a solution to their search.

CAMPAIGN: Brand Search Campaigns

The age-old serviced accommodation marketing debate: Should you bid on your own brand name or not?

The simple answer is *yes*. The question should not be whether to bid on your brand; it should be whether you can afford not to!

Most apartment operators rely on OTA's to help them drive business and offer a billboard effect for their brand. However, direct bookings are always best. They come at a lower CPA, encourage loyalty and give you the opportunity to upsell.

Brand campaigns on the search network allow you to show your ads to users actively searching for your hotel. The casual traveller is often clueless about the channel or website the complete this booking on, so advertising a 'guaranteed best rate when you book direct 'is a strong way to persuade them that direct is the best channel for them.

Additionally, it makes sure you appear near the top of search results. If you're on OTA's, it's highly likely that they're running ads on your brand name. Don't let them appear first for *your* brand!

Your ads allow you to ensure your direct channel is front and centre of the user's search, with the ad text clearly outlining the benefits to book direct.

Metrics to Watch

CPA, or Cost per Acquisition, is the most important metric with brand search campaigns. Are these campaigns returning a lower CPA than bookings on another channel?

Secondly, look at engagement with the landing page for your campaign – the page that your ads direct users to. You should look at bounce rate, time on page, and the number of pages per session those users have on your site. Are they only looking at the landing page, or are they moving on to the booking engine or the rest of your site?

Finally, what's the ROI for your campaign overall? Was the profit worth it?

CAMPAIGN: Generic Search Campaigns

Staying on the search network, generic search campaigns allow you to reach users at the 'prospecting 'or 'shopping ' stage of the purchase funnel.

Think of long tail keyword searches from users aiming to find accommodation which meets their needs: *'Southampton apartment with jacuzzi'*, or *'short term rental near Dublin train station'*

Needless the say, when the user is closer to the top of the booking funnel, these campaigns are costlier and are harder to convert. However, if you have a strong offering and you land the user in on an engaging landing page experience, generic campaigns allow you to drive traffic from users who would have perhaps never found your brand.

Generic search campaigns benefit significantly when other sequential campaigns are in place. A combination of booking funnel remarketing and display remarketing work best. These help ensure that once you have paid for the user to visit your website, you do everything possible to ensure they return to book.

Metrics to Watch

Keep an eye on engagement with the advertisement (click through rate, or CTR, is a good KPI) and landing page engagement, including bounce rate, time on page, etc.

As before, you should also pay attention to ROI and CPA.

THE DISPLAY NETWORK

The Google display network (GDN) consists of millions of websites, news pages, blogs, and Google websites like Gmail and YouTube. The Google Display Network reaches 90% of Internet users worldwide. (*Source: Google*)

Advertising on the 'Display 'network is often called "interruption marketing," as it "interrupts" the viewer whilst they are browsing the web. In that sense, it's the opposite of search advertisements, which show up when the user is actively searching on Google.

To have a successful display campaign, your strategy must be different to search campaigns. Importantly, your adverts and landing pages need to be carefully thought out.

CAMPAIGN: Remarketing on the Google Display Network

In simple terms, remarketing lists allow you to target users who have already engaged with certain content on your website based on a set of criteria. In other words, you're not simply reaching out to people who've never encountered your brand, so you have a much stronger chance of getting conversions.

For example, one list may collect all users within a 30-day window who have visited your website, entered the booking funnel, yet didn't yet complete a booking.

For this audience, we know they have been interested in booking your accommodation, yet for some reason they didn't complete. This might have happened because they weren't sure yet, because they got distracted, or even just because they didn't have their credit card on hand.

Here are a few ways to combat booking abandonment. One of those ways is, of course, remarketing.

Showing adverts to these users which promote your brand and remind them why they should book allows you to stay front and centre while they are in the decision process.

Tip: Eliminating anyone who has already completed their booking is important for these campaigns, so that your message reaches the correct audience. Make sure your audience excludes anyone who has, for example, reached the 'Thank You for Booking 'page on your website.

For Display campaigns, both image and animated adverts tend to perform better than text adverts.

Metrics to Watch

Keep an eye on engagement with the advertisement (CTR) and landing page engagement, including bounce rate, time on page, etc.

As before, you should also pay attention to ROI and CPA, with a special focus on view through conversions and direct conversions.

CAMPAIGN: Generic Display Campaigns

Generic Display campaigns are at the top end of the funnel and fall under 'prospecting'. Often, the key strategy for display campaigns is to drive brand awareness to an audience of users who have not engaged with your brand before, but who might be interested.

Knowing where and how your existing audience engages with your brand is more important than ever. This information should mould your display campaign strategies. The data in Google Analytics can arm you with everything you need to know here, from demographics to audience interests.

Equally important is ensuring the message is precise and landing page is highly relevant to your target audience. A vague or bland campaign will have little impact on your audience, and if you don't have a compelling landing page, you risk losing their interest immediately.

When creating display campaigns, your ads can be matched to websites that include content that's related to your business or to your customers 'interests. You can set up targeting to match your ads based on topics, interested audiences, user demographics, and more.

Metrics to Watch

As above, keep an eye on engagement with the advertisement, but you should also look at where these campaigns fall in your conversion funnel. Since they're often more about brand awareness than specifically driving bookings, CTR is less important here. Instead, look at where they lie in your attribution model.

As before, you should also pay attention to ROI and CPA, with a special focus on view through conversions.

THE VIDEO NETWORK

The video network is the most under-utilised network by the serviced accommodation industry, primarily due to the lack of **quality and relevant videos** available at the apartment level.

A strong video doesn't have to cost a lot to produce, and it doesn't need to be 15 minutes long – in fact, it shouldn't! If you have an iPhone, a tripod and a sunny day, you're well on your way. You can use your professional photos, and some stock videos to make an informative one minute video.

Shorter is better than longer, and small topics are better than big ones. I would recommend that serviced apartment operators create 4 separate videos for different business areas, rather than 1 longer generic video.

For example, you might want a video for your local events, your corporate business and one to show off your surrounding areas or landmarks. Another brand might swap corporate business for families, or add in a video about their spa or gold course vouchers if that's what you want to offer.

Ideally you're creating videos that are short, sweet and to the point, with a clear message and call to action. Anything from 20-40 seconds would be recommended. The great thing about videos is that once you have videos created, you can use them across multiple platforms – social platforms, your website, and of course the video network.

Some video stats:

Over half of video content is viewed on mobile. Make sure the video makes sense without sound and don't include microscopic text.

51% of marketing professionals worldwide name video as the type of content with the best ROI.

Marketers who use video grow revenue 49% faster than non-video users.

CAMPAIGN: Video 136

Just as we do with Display remarketing, we suggest hotels run video remarketing. It's a super engaging way to showcase your serviced apartment brand to someone who has just been on your website.

A relevant video to this audience can help to reinforce your **USP** or **Book Direct message** just that little bit more effectively than an image or text advert.

It's important that the video:

- Is relevant to the audience
- Has a clear call to action

- Has a strong landing page experience

Metrics to Watch

As always, keep an eye on engagement with the advertisement (in this case, how long are they watching the video, and are they clicking through?) and landing page engagement, including bounce rate, time on page, etc.

As before, you should also pay attention to ROI and CPA, with a special focus on view through conversions and direct conversions.

Conclusion

From my perspective, these are the 5 most important types of campaigns to run on **Google AdWords for the serviced apartment industry.**

Google AdWords is a powerful tool, and your brand needs to have it as a major part of their marketing strategy to be truly competitive. Hopefully, even if you don't work with a digital marketing agency, this section will give you the right tools to start promoting your brand on Google Ads.

Facebook

We are in the midst of a social marketing revolution, and there are huge new opportunities for growth. Facebook in particular is a powerful platform for driving direct bookings for your brand.

Your guests have changed, and are now more digitally aware and involved in the research and booking process.

They are engaged in every step of the process, and this puts them in the driving seat more than ever before.

We need to understand new ways to connect with potential guests, with the kind of depth and colour they're now used to.

This section will give you a crash course in selling your brand on Facebook, and will help you understand the key principles of social media that will enable you to turn social media into bookings. Not every channel or tool is right for every STR brand! It's important to test and choose the ones that suit and work best for your property. Figure out where your target audience is spending their time online and ensure you have an engaged presence there.

Social networking sites have revolutionised the way we use the internet today: if you don't have an active social media presence, you simply don't exist. You are missing out on huge opportunities to engage and sell to your existing and potential guests. According to Adweek.com, the average user logs about 1.78 hours per day on social platforms, accounting for 28% of all their online activity.

So why not take just a little slice of that online activity and use it to your benefit? You can take advantage of social to drive direct bookings for your business.

Optimising your Facebook

Presence

Facebook often update their algorithms to ensure that its users are getting the best possible experience each time that they log in. It's getting increasingly harder for your brand's business page to stand out in all the noise.

In order to be on top of your game, let's look at a few optimisation tips.

1: Profile and Cover Photos

Ensure that your profile pictures and cover photos represent your brand and are reflective of your brand's website. You don't want to have a cartoonish profile picture or an outdated logo on your page; make sure your pictures on Facebook are as polished as your site and match it in tone.

Take a look at this handy cheat sheet by John Loomer to ensure that all of your images are optimised for every possible outcome.

https://www.jonloomer.com/2015/05/11/facebook-image-dimensions-2015/

2. Fill out the About Us

Your About Us section should be as full as possible. Make sure that you have a link directly back to your brand website. Information like how guests can get in touch with you and where you are located are vital.

3. Create a Vanity URL

A custom Facebook url, e.g

facebook.com/mycitypod, gives you the opportunity to enhance your brand recognition. It also holds high value in search rankings, making it easier for guests to find when they do a search.

4. Optimise your brand's Facebook page for SEO

- Facebook social signals can have a lot of potential for SEO value – use it as a channel to build traffic and links back to your brand website.

- Harness the power of the graph search: use keywords in your content and page updates. Graph search is a semantic search engine that was introduced to the Facebook platform in 2013. It searches content across the platform, and serves up keyword results based on the user's network.

- Take advantage of the customised meta titles and images when you share links in your posts. Facebook will automatically pull in images and titles from your website to display in a carousel like post – however, you can choose which images you wish to upload and edit the text.

- Share high-quality content that will generate engagement such as likes, comments & shares.

If you find that you're stuck for time to generate good content, you might want to consider **scheduling your posts**. Scheduling your posts will save you time as you can batch your work. Posts can be scheduled anywhere from 10 minutes before to 6 months ahead, so you've got a lot of flexibility.

You can schedule your posts directly from your Facebook timeline by clicking on the dropdown arrow under your post.

source: facebook.com

Alternatively, you can create your schedule posts in bulk from the publishing tools section:

You can use a content calendar like the one we've provided below to help you to plan out your Facebook activity to help you to save time. This will also give you the opportunity to see where you may have gaps in your content, and let you to look back at posts that perform well for you.

5. Use Interest Targeting

Use your fans 'interests to target specific parts of your audience. to reach specific fans and narrow your audience – base your content on your key personas to include demographic, location and interests targeting for your organic posts.

6. Use of the Call To Action Button

Below are samples of serviced accommodation brands that are using their calls to action for direct bookings and email newsletter sign ups. Other uses might include Shop Now, Watch Video & Contact Us.

Soure: https://www.facebook.com/staycity

Source: https://www.facebook.com/MarlinApartmentsCanaryWharf

7. Enable Ratings and Reviews

To activate reviews on your Facebook page, you must have a **local business listing** and have your full business address featured in the about us section.

8. Use Rich Media in the Newsfeed

Create an experience that potential guests want to engage with.

Move away from sharing simple text links with thumbnails. It's time to get creative! Jazz up your posts with bright imagery and video clips uploaded directly to the Facebook platform.

9. Use Apps to Customise

Facebook apps allow you to customise your page in many ways. Take a step back from your Facebook page, and ask yourself: What are you doing that's engaging and keeping your brand's fans on your Facebook page?

- **Competition apps**: using competition apps allows for tons of flexibility in the information that you can collect from fans, and it keeps them engaged and prevents them from leaving the platform.

- **Email captures:** Add a sign-up form tab. Offer an incentive for guests to sign up to your newsletter. Once you've collected your list, use it to retarget potential guests with special offers and packages to book direct on your brand's site.

10. Make shareable, fresh content

Make sure you have a steady stream of **shareable content on your website** – keep your content up to date. Not only is fresh content helpful from a social media perspective, but it will also benefit you from a search engine optimisation point of view and engage guests that find their way to your site. Fresh content is a win-win-win.

11. Add social sharing icons

Ensure that your content is easily shareable to Facebook and other platforms– add social sharing icons to your website with easy tools like ShareThis, AddThis or SumoMe.

12. Look at who your audience is

Learn more about the customers that matter to you before you invest in paid advertising with Facebook Audience Insights. Audience Insights give you information about your fans like demographic, location, interests, connections and more – think of it as a mini-Google Analytics for your Facebook page.

Yes, you can customise your target audience with adverts manager before setting your campaigns live. What if you could learn more about your specific audience before putting budget behind it, though?

Audience Insights were developed to help you learn more about your target markets by looking at trends about your current and potential customers based on real time data. It will allow you to view information about three groups of people:

- People on Facebook

- People connected to your page or event

- People in custom audiences which you may have already created, e.g. an e-mail database or a custom audience collected from your website.

Let's say you want to target male and females between the ages of 35-44 in the UK who are interested in Airbnb and are frequent travellers. In the example below, you will notice that you are now targeting 65% of women and 35% of men, 62% of whom are married and 67% of which are educated to college level. Looking at this further, we can see that 39% of this audience have a Management type job title.

You don't have access to this type of information outside of this tool. This will help you to tailor your ad copy based on analysis. For example, this particular audience may be more affluent and would be more inclined to spend on a break away, and with the majority of the audience being married, you might want to target them with couples' packages.

Once you have analysed specific information about your customers you can then save this specific audience and use it as a target audience at a later stage.

Job Title

Job Title	Selected Audience		Compare ▾
Life, Physical and Social Sciences	12%	▬▬▬▬▬▬▬▬	+47%
IT and Technical Services	13%	▬▬▬▬▬▬▬▬	+42%
Computation and Mathematics	13%	▬▬▬▬▬▬▬▬	+42%
Management	39%	▬▬▬▬▬▬▬▬▬▬▬▬▬▬▬▬▬▬	+36%
Government Employees (Global)	0.4%	▎	+33%
Arts, Entertainment, Sports and Media	16%	▬▬▬▬▬▬▬▬▬▬	+33%
Community and Social Services	8%	▬▬▬▬▬	+31%
Education and Libraries	10%	▬▬▬▬▬▬	+25%
Legal Services	2%	▬	+25%
Business and Finance	13%	▬▬▬▬▬▬▬▬	+24%

13. Use Paid Advertising

Facebook advertising should be an essential part of your brand digital marketing strategy to drive direct bookings back to your own brand site. Facebook often update their algorithms to ensure users receive the best-personalised experience each time they log in.

The news feed is at the center of Facebook success – Facebook serves up posts to user that they are more likely to engage with. This is great news for users, but more of a challenge for us marketers to compete for real estate in this ever-more competitive environment.

Lately, you may have noticed a drop in your posts 'organic reach. This is because of Facebook's algorithm update in January 2015 and 2017, makes it near-impossible to rely on organic reach alone without the backup of paid advertising. Organic reach refers to the number of people that you can reach on Facebook for free by posting on your page. In order to gain as much exposure as possible, let's take a quick look at the paid options that are available to you and will best help to drive direct bookings.

Boosted Posts

Boosting your posts is an extremely effective and inexpensive way to get as much exposure as possible for your content. It's a simple way to get more relevant people to see your posts allowing you to choose a specific audience to target for a set budget over a set period of time. Boosted posts appear higher in the newsfeed, so there is a much better chance that your audience will see and engage with them.

Unpublished Page Posts or "Ghost Posts"

Unpublished page posts are used solely for the purpose of advertising and don't appear on your brand's Facebook page or in news feeds. They are an effective way to show your content to **a tailored audience** and allow you to display a call to action button.

Custom Audiences

Facebook's custom audiences allow you to reach customers you already have an established relationship with. These types of campaigns are super-effective, and avoid the wasted clicks you'd get from a more generic audience.

Website custom audience

Collect a list of people who have visited specific pages on your website. You can start collating this list as soon as you add the Facebook custom audience pixel across your website. For example, you may want to target people who have checked availability on your website but who haven't proceeded to the booking stage. These people are the low-hanging fruit, and worth retargeting through Facebook to entice them to come back to book directly on your website.

Email / Phone number Retargeting

You can upload a list of at least 20 email addresses or phone numbers directly to Facebook, and it will automatically match these up with the relevant Facebook IDs if they are on Facebook.

This targeting is very useful when you use it alongside an existing campaign. For example, you may want to retarget people whom you have sent an e-mail to in the past couple of days. It is important here to exclude the people who have actually booked as a result of receiving your e-mails or newsletter.

Lookalike Audiences

Lookalike audiences allow you to target and reach new people who are similar to one of your custom audiences. For example, a powerful lookalike audience would be people similar to those who've already made a booking on your website. Facebook will then match up the top % of users to display your ads to.

Advanced Targeting

There are numerous advanced targeting options that can

be layered on top on one another, gradually making your audience smaller and more relevant, driving down costs and raising ROI. You can use single factors or combinations of interests, behaviours & geo location.

Take a look at the following:

How many people or 'gurus' have you seen in groups trouting Facebook ads for direct bookings? Many, right? And how many have explained the strategy behind it? None! Because most of these gurus just use buzz words to trigger people into buying their hype. Think about it; when you go on Facebook, do you go on there to be sold to, or do you go there to socialize and look at cat videos and gym fail emes? Im betting it's the latter. Even if you were planning a holiday, are you going to book 'Steven's' (Steven is a fictious character I made up) apartment simply because you've seen it advertised on FB? NO! Because Steven's apartment is probably not in the location you want to travel to, it's not big enough and it's probably not available for your dates! Now imagine a marketer running ads to millions of people and saying "we got a lot of bookings from FB". How silly does that sound now?

When running Facebook ads, don't expect people to see your ad, and then book straight away. Every traveller goes through five stages called 'micro-moments before they finally book accommodation for holiday or business. Before making this investment, travellers are taking time to research all the possibilities. Over 40% of travellers say they bounce back and forth between dreaming about and planning their next trip—zooming in on the details for one destination and then zooming out to reconsider all the options again.

And more and more of this time is spent researching the details of trips on mobile. As more research happens in the traveler's customer journey, there are more micro-moments—when people turn to a device with intent to answer an immediate need. In these moments, the stakes are high for travel brands like us, as preferences are shaped and decisions are made. What happens in these micro-moments ultimately affects the travel decision-making process.

The 4 stages that travellers go through before making a decision are:

Inspiration- these are the moments when a traveller realise that they want or need to travel. Travellers at this point are looking at different options in multiple destinations

Planning- this is the stage where they are actively making plans and honing down on options in a particular destination.

Booking- this is the stage where they have found a destination and are now ready to book accommodation that meets their immediate requirements e.g. price, availability, proximity to the reason they are booking. For example, how far is the accommodation to 'Lego Land' or an exhibition centre.

Exploring- you may think that a secured booking is the end of the road when it comes to serving travellers' needs. But providing useful information in these particular micro-moments is a way to build your brand, drive word of mouth, and increase loyalty among travellers.

Now that you understand the journey of a traveller before they book accommodation, you might be wondering which moment Facebook ads advanced targeting comes into play? The answer is Facebook plays a key part in the Planning and Booking moments, that's because Facebook ads allow us to target a specific group of people, based on their behaviour. Facebook now has 1.69 billion users so as you can imagine, running a blanket, basic advert without targeting properly will be very expensive and yield no results. Below is an example of how I would target people who travel to Manchester regularly:

The objective I would pick is 'Traffic' Because we want the user to click on my advert and go to my website to sign up to my newletter: Remember the rule of direct marketing' there will always be an offer' *See figure below*

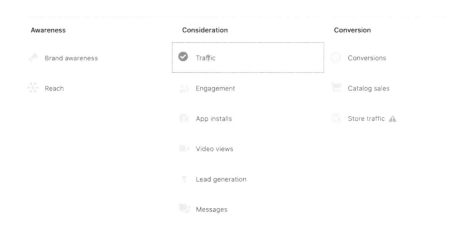

Then next, you need to make use of Facebook's feature

where you reach people who are intending to travel. *See following figure*:

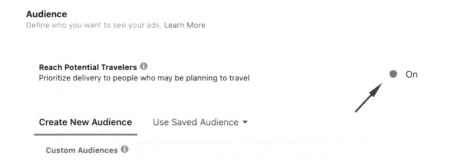

Then create your audience by selecting ' **People travelling in this location'**

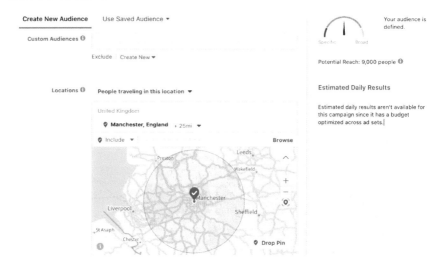

Build your audience by selecting relevant age groups, gender, interests and behaviours

As you can see, the audience I have created is:

Men and women aged between 27- 50 who travel to

Manchester regularly for business. They also frequent websites like Airbnb and booking.com

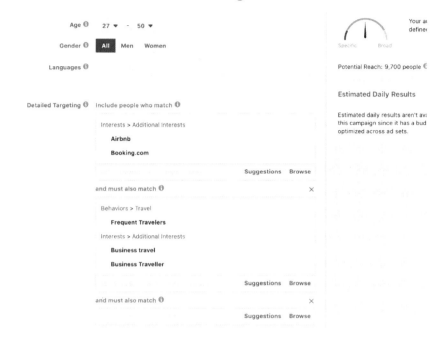

This audience would give me a much better conversion rate than an advert targeting everyone on Facebook who like Airbnb and booking.com, can you see how powerful Facebook ads are?

Your guests spend most of their time on Facebook, it's the cheapest form of advertising, it's fast and drives immediate results if you use it for list building, it's measurable and can drive repeat business. Why would you not utilise it as part of your direct booking strategy?

Conclusion

There are always new ways for you to reach out to potential guests, and Facebook is just one of the platforms that you can use to develop long-lasting relationships. You need to make an effort to engage with your fans, listen to what they have to say and get ahead of your competition.

Remember not to oversell on every Facebook post! Keep the 80/20 rule in mind: only 20% of your content should be about your brand, and the other 80% should be dedicated to sharing content that really matters to your audience and engages with them in conversations.

TripAdvisor (the truth)

When TripAdvisor was founded in February 2000 in a small office above Kostas Pizza on 315 Chestnut Street in Needham, Massachusetts, I don't think anyone could have predicted the amount of time and energy it would consume, and the strong emotions it would conjure.

Since I started my consulting in 2017, I have consistently fielded questions about TripAdvisor. Looking back at the sheer volume of time I spent answering these complex emails, I think it's time to for me aggregate my knowledge, experience and advice in one place. Here are some of the most frequently asked questions, along with my responses.

Is my competition trying to take my business down on TripAdvisor?

Short Answer: Yes, it's possible.

Long Answer: I get asked about this a lot by around the world. "You are not being paranoid" is how I start most replies. There are some hotel owners/operators who turn to the dark side when it comes to TripAdvisor. Instead of improving their own product and service, they trash their competition. These are the folks that the youth today refer to as the haters.

The hospitality industry has always had its fair share of bad apples. Anytime you claim something is powered by algorithms, there will be a group of players ready to game the system. In a time when so much power is bestowed upon TripAdvisor, a lot of time people feel desperate to win. Desperation should lead to hard work...but often leads instead to a "win by any means" mentality. How many hotels SA operators walk on the dark side by writing/sponsoring their own glowing reviews and/or posting negative ones for their competitors will never truly be known.

Offenders are not just mom and pop operations. Let's not forget Peter Hook*, a senior executive at Accor Hotels who took it upon himself to write awesome reviews for his own hotels while posting negative ones for competing brands. He got caught when the TripAdvisor Facebook app linked his anonymous username "Travare" to his Facebook account – after he had posted 106 reviews in 43 cities!

This incident happened all the way back in 2013... so how have things changed? Elementary, Watson. The bad guys have gotten much smarter.

*Self-fulfilling prophecy: He described himself in his Twitter bio as the "Director of Propaganda" for Accor hotels in Asia-Pacific.

Can you game the TripAdvisor "algorithm"?

Short answer: Yes.

Long answer: It has been done, and has led to some epic fails for TripAdvisor.

- Bellgrove Hotel, Glasgow. In 2013, this "hotel heaven," a hostel for the homeless, made it onto the list of TripAdvisor's 100 best places to stay, thanks to the efforts of pranksters who posted numerous five-star reviews.

- La Scaletta, Italy. Italians know their food, fashion and automobiles. Apparently they also know how to expose the flawed "algorithms" of the largest review site in the world. Read how a non-existent restaurant made it to the #1 spot. I gotta give it to the Italians on this one...the phone number for the restaurant was that of the city's police station! Prendere in giro! The final burn: In December 2014, the Italian Antitrust Authority fined TripAdvisor €500,000, complaining that the site had failed to adopt controls to stop false reviews while promoting its content as "authentic and genuine."

- The Shed at Dulwich, South London. All the British food jokes aside, London now has a ton of exciting chefs and restaurants competing for dominance in a growing food and beverage scene. Enter freelance writer Oobah Butler. His fake restaurant in South London became "London's Top Rated Restaurant" on TripAdvisor. And this was all happening in 2017, not that long ago.

- The Riu Imperial Marhaba, Tunisia. This story is really tragic. Thirty-eight people were shot at this hotel, and it had closed its operations. Yet TripAdvisor included it on its coveted "2016 Traveler's Choice Award" list. Makes you wonder, when do you become too big to do basic research when making your award lists?

PSA: Don't put your life in the hands of a review site.

Let's take a brief moment to address something terrifying about TripAdvisor: Profits will always be more important than people.

For me, the darkest side of TripAdvisor's unchecked power and accountability was exposed in 2017 by The Milwaukee Journal, which uncovered how reports of rape and assault at some all-inclusive resorts in Mexico were deleted from their site. These two publicly posted excerpts really highlight the problem:

Exhibit A:

Milwaukee Journal: Why were these warnings deleted?

TripAdvisor: They were "determined to be inappropriate by the TripAdvisor community," or removed by staff because they were "off-topic" or contained language or subject matter that was not "family friendly."

The Milwaukee Journal Sentinel asked to see the posts that were removed. The company refused.

Exhibit B:

When there were murmurs that the US Federal Trade Commission would be getting involved, TripAdvisor put out an official response via The Verge and Engadget. Here is an excerpt:

"We are not aware of an inquiry by the Federal Trade Commission nor have they contacted us. TripAdvisor is a global user-generated content platform that enables travellers to post positive and negative reviews and forum content about their experiences. We receive 290 pieces of content a minute and need to ensure that information posted on our site adheres to our content guidelines to ensure the integrity of these posts. We stand by our publishing guidelines and how they are applied."

What I heard:

1. The FTC is not coming after us, we are funded and have tons of cash for lawyers, so all is good with us.

2. We get 290 pieces of content/minute for free. You really think we should be expected to hire enough people to go through it?

3. We stand by our "publishing guidelines"... too bad about your death, robbery and sexual assault.

4. Now if you'll excuse us, we will go back to selling ads to hotels and restaurants.

The fact of the matter is, when you book a room at a hotel and make the decision solely based on the "world's largest review site," you are sometimes taking your life into your own hands. Remember, just as with Facebook: it's a free site and they owe you absolutely nothing.

Do you use TripAdvisor to research personal travel?

People on my email list ask me a ton of personal questions. Should I feel like a celebrity? Short answer: No.

Whether or not I personally use TripAdvisor is a common question. Yes, I do. But, like anyone who does research on TripAdvisor, I've had to learn how to analyse what I'm seeing. I almost feel like Sherlock Holmes when I am reading a hotel or restaurant's TripAdvisor page, looking for clues and using astute observation to determine what's really going on.

I do not have a degree in psychology or behavioural sciences, but I have to say that I am a Quantico-level fake hotel review spotter. The sheer number of hours I have spent on TripAdvisor has given me almost perfect clarity. I feel like Neo in The Matrix...making the bullets slow all the way down. (Here is a link for some of you young readers.) The fact is that anyone (with a little practice) can spot the low-quality reviews posted by competitors, tricksters and desperate owners.

Here is my typical process, in case you want to sharpen your own methods:

Look Beyond the Algorithm. I check to see how heavily the provider is investing in TripAdvisor advertising. The amount of money a provider is spending on TripAdvisor advertising equates to how much time, energy and money is NOT getting spent on things that matter.

Example: I can see when a brand general manager's bonus has been tied into their TripAdvisor rankings. That means the GM is spending a ton of time online, instead of the reception talking to guests. As a user, you need to realise that TripAdvisor stars and rankings are guidelines, not commandments. To find real value, you have to dig deeper than the surface and play with the price and location filters. As with any set of data, you have to segment to win.

1. **Are They Trying Too Hard?** I look out for providers that press too hard for you to leave reviews online, offer special prices in exchange for reviews, etc. When a brand steps into desperation mode, you know a lot of time and energy is going into collecting the volume of reviews and not the quality of the product itself. I have seen it all...from brands offering to "complete" the review for me, to them sending me 10 emails requesting a review, to placing TripAdvisor review cards in the W/C. Remember folks: Desperation is never attractive.

2. **'Everything Is Awesome.'** Oh, great... I now have that song from the Lego movie stuck in my head! These providers are easy to spot because everything there is awesome. It is impossible to run a hotel type of business that is all things to all people. When I see a barrage of awesome reviews non-stop over a short period of time, it pretty much signals that there is something going on that deserves more scrutiny.

3. **Go Direct.** What do I do when I have a question/doubt? Email the operator. It's easy. Click on the contact page and reach out to a real human who might be able to answer questions, make recommendations, etc. Believe it or not, it works 99% of the time! If you do not have a positive experience doing this, you will know what's behind the curtain of the TripAdvisor reviews and rankings.

4. **Diversify.** TripAdvisor is not the only review site out there. Don't forget the little search engine that is out to take everyone's lunch. Google's hotel reviews are a good source for quick concise content. Before I dive into TripAdvisor and start psychoanalysing their "trusted" reviews, while getting hit with terrible banner ads and being yelled at to "book the best deal I will ever see in my whole damn life"... I locate the brand on Google and see if there are some usable reviews. Let's not forget there are a ton of professional travellers that post some truly amazing long-form hotel reviews.

5. **Log Off.** Last but not the least. Friends don't let friends browse TripAdvisor while logged into their account! Right now is a pretty bad time for privacy. Let's not divulge more information about ourselves to a multibillion dollar corporation! You don't need them to serve you more "targeted" banner ads that you ignore, while they are heavily pushing us to buy these useless ads. TripAdvisor's "Just For You"

recommendations is not a feature designed to make your life better...it's an avenue to sell more ads.

PSA #2: TripAdvisor's homepage tagline evolution tells a story.

There is no hiding the fact that American companies love their taglines. TripAdvisor went after the whole *trust* thing hard for the longest time, until trade law finally caught up with them.

2006: "Get the Truth. Then Go."

2010: "World's most trusted travel advice"

2011: (April) "Over 45 million trusted traveler reviews & opinions"

2011: (September) TripAdvisor is banned from claiming that their reviews are "trustworthy" and must remove the following phrases from their website, courtesy of British Advertising Standards Authority:

- "Read real reviews from real travellers"

- "Reviews you can trust"

- "More than 50 million honest travel reviews and opinions from travellers around the world"

2013: "The World's Largest Travel Site" (The word "trust" is completely gone.)

2018: "The world's largest travel site. Know better. Book better. Go better."

Are TripAdvisor's sponsored placements and ads a good idea?

Note: This is probably the most common question I get.

Short answer: No

Long Answer: Don't pay to drive traffic to OTAs. They definitely don't need your help making more money. If you need "brand exposure," invest in your service and product instead. Investing in impressions and click-based ads on a platform that is not connected exclusively to your website and booking engine defies logic. Unless you are P&G/Unilever/General Electric with money to burn...spending money on banner impressions is a huge waste of your marketing dollars. In 2019 I spent over £1,000 on the Business Advantage subscription and I can honestly say it was a waste of money and time. We had two direct bookings that totalled £270, we also ran some sponsored ads and those amounted to nothing, however we were still paying for the clicks, which are actually more expensive than Google's PPC ads.

"Logic is the beginning of wisdom ... not the end."

How about you invest in these 5 things instead:

1. Make a better hospitality website- the quickest way to get started is to find a Wordpress theme on ThemeForest.net and get someone on Fiverr to customise it. That shouldn't cost you more than£100!

2. Invest in better apartment content and photos- as I mentioned in previous chapters, hire a professional

property photographer, dress the apartment and get amazing photos taken. If you are bad at writing, again, hire someone from Fiverr or PPH to write your website content. Just make sure you use some or all of the rules at the top of this chapter to make sure it's copy that sells your rooms.

3. Get a better booking engine- some Wordpress themes will come with a booking engine that has the iCal feature which is great, if it hasn't, just ensure you sign up to a channel manager that offer a booking engine. That way guests can book instantly and you can avoid over-bookings.

4. Improve your product value- These days it's not enough to just list 'an apartment' for booking. Guests are more demanding and are on the look out for value, and in most cases, value doesn't always equate to low pricing. Something as simple as car parking space or welcome pack with breakfast essentials can be enough to tip the scales in your favour.

5. Invest on Google, and drive direct traffic- Invest on Google ads to drive direct traffic to your website. Only do this when you have a booking engine that displays all the rates for the entire year as shoppers can book last minute or up to six months in advance. If your channel manager has a Google Hotel Integration, then this can run alongside your Google Ads. You don't need to do any work with this because the channel manager will display your accommodation to someone who's looking for

accommodation automatically, if you have availability. This is what it looks like to the user if you have connected your property to GHA:

Example: guest types in Google 'short stay apartments Bracknell'

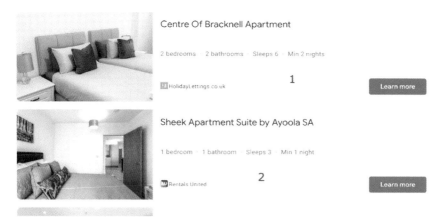

The photo above reflects results that would come up on the results page of Google. As you can see OTAs and Listing websites like HolidayLettings also place your properties on Google Hotel Ads. Up until 2018, this privilege was only available to big OTAs and hotel websites, however small brands can now list their properties there as well. If you look at the photo above, the property I've tagged '2' takes part in GHA. United Rentals is a channel manager that they use to enable the connectivity. If a user clicks on 'Learn more' they are taken to a dedicated Google page for the brand, and if the user wants to make a booking, they are taken to the brand's website where they complete the booking using the booking engine. Simple, yet an extremely effective and affordable way to drive direct bookings as you are only charged a commission when a booking is confirmed.

What do you think of the good ol ꞌTripAdvisor business listing?

Short Answer: This prehistoric marketing tactic by which you spend money for a link, which is declining in volume every year, deserves to be in a marketing museum.

Long Answer: I am old enough to remember when TripAdvisor launched their infamous Business Listing for hotels.

Fast forward to 2020. TripAdvisor still successfully charges a lot of money for placing a link to your brand website. I must hand it to their marketing machine for showcasing the yuge value of this link. The word "convenience" gets thrown around a lot. How helpless are guests that they cannot open another tab in their browser and just Google the brand that has piqued their interest on TripAdvisor?

Here is the kicker. Over the past several years, the volume of traffic from a TripAdvisor business listing has dropped across the board for all brands that I have worked with, including mine. The success of the new TripConnect CPC and InstantBook products has something to do with this. Why sell you a click for just a flat fee? Why not make a % commission on top of it by converting those clicks. The whole convenience argument starts to fall apart when you realise that anyone booking travel in this day and age has at least 5-10 tabs open on their browser.

So I cannot understand why brands would continue to pay for a simple link to their website from a page on a third party site. Possible answers:

- **Convenience.** You really think someone smart enough to read online reviews cannot open a new tab in their browser and Google you? Spending thousands of pounds every year to save your guest a click?

- **Fear.** There is heavy speculation that your TripAdvisor rankings' allegedly 'might decline when you stop advertising with them. Lawyers, pay attention that I am using the word "allegedly."

- **Habit.** There is the "we have always done this and it's now a part of our annual budget" reasoning. An average hotel in London is probably paying 10K to 15K for a link. Now imagine they took that cash and spent it on better coffee for guests in their lobby. Or how about renting puppies to hang out with the guests on weekends? Imagine the possibilities! I hope you get the point I'm making with this. Don't get caught up in the whole 'brand advertising' type of marketing, It's expensive, it doesn't yield results, and it doesn't work! Trust me, I learned the hard way.

Do I have to promote my new SA with TripAdvisor Sponsored Ads?

Short answer: No.

Long Answer: Here is a simple two-question test you can use to find the answer for yourself.

Question 1. Is the ego of the owner/operator tied to TripAdvisor rankings?

Then yes, you will have to run banner ads on TripAdvisor, get little or no reporting in return, and listen to someone talk about Billboard Effect in your marketing meetings. Everyone will be pleased and there will be high fives all around.

Question 2. Is the owner/operator a professional who wants to generate net operating income while offering a good product?

Then no, there are better options for promoting a new serviced apartments brand (especially if you have 5or more). You need to perfect your product first and then grow organically. Organic growth is much more permanent than plastering the internet with banner ads that nobody cares for. In addition, you need to target guests at several different points in the buying cycle. There are many other channels where you can list your business and get exposure, just to get a baseline on your newly opened product. There is even this little billion-dollar hotel booking site out of Amsterdam (booking.com) and another one in Bellevue (Expedia) than can help you get exposure without annoying people with sponsored listings.

Are your revenue and TripAdvisor rankings related?

Short answer: Yes.

Long answer: There is no denying that your revenue is going to take a hit if you lose your rankings. But please understand that it is not the end of the world. To make a profit, you must diversify. Google, Expedia and Booking all have reviews too; don't put all your review eggs in one basket. Recovery from a TripAdvisor meltdown is possible, but your pricing, marketing and product quality need to be in full alignment. Please do not tie your distribution to a review website. That way, when the TripAdvisor "algorithm" is not your favour, the odds might still be in your favour. Get it?

Pro tip: Do not tie your personal sanity to TripAdvisor. Stay focused on the real world and engage with your guests in real time. The saddest thing I've seen in relation to TripAdvisor was at a trade show. A hotel owner was in tears pleading with TripAdvisor staff, saying that his negative reviews were affecting his marriage. Don't be that guy; don't give so much emotional power to a review website!

Conclusion

TripAdvisor is a social media network that uses free content to make money. Your brand is a physical brick and mortar business in the real world that people can experience by booking a stay. Before you know it, someone will acquire TripAdvisor; then the new owners will figure out more ways to increase their bottom line. You cannot obsess over it, or automatically spend your hard-earned revenue on buying advertising without thinking it through. You are not in high school anymore. In the long term, it really does not matter what people say about you. Run a good short term rental business, work hard, be kind to your guests, and it's inevitable that you will make money!

Branding your short term rental

In this branding section, we're taking a look at the three cornerstones of short term rental brands—your approach to guests, your location, and your property's signature vibe—and showing you how to leverage these to create a recognisable, relatable brand that calls to your ideal guests.

So, let's talk branding for short rental businesses.

As the industry grows and changes (100% growth since 2014!), we hear a lot about the importance of branding. But what exactly *is* a brand?

(Hint: it's more than just your rental company's logo.)

Laying the groundwork for your short term rental brand means considering these three essential factors:

1. Your approach to guests
2. The location of your rental(s) and what it has that the neighbours don't
3. The characteristic vibe your rental gives to guests

We'll talk about all three in-depth in this branding series—and give you strategies for leveraging these three factors to create a brand that helps your ideal guests recognise you as the perfect choice for their stay.

But before we get there, first let me tell you something important: your short term rental *already* has a brand. Whether you know it or not.

You make countless decisions every day at your rental.

What brand of towels do we use in the bathroom? What's our policy for responding to negative reviews? What website design will best capture your rentals 'unique vibe?

All of these small and large decisions add up to your *brand*. The key is to figure out what all of these decisions have in common. And then formalise it and stay true to it in everything your short term rental business puts out in the world—including, yes, your logo, but also your guest communications, your social media presence, and your website.

Let's say you have an impressive secluded barn conversion with acres of untouched land surrounding it.

You might think building a decent website that boasts of its amenities and bedroom configuration is enough. But to truly tap into guests 'emotions, you can create a brand that establishes your rental as a whimsical escape under the stars, where you'll spend time sitting around the campfire and exploring nature with the ones you love.

What sounds more convincing—booking a high-end rental or signing on for an unforgettable family experience deep in the woods?

Branding gets you from the former to the latter.

So what is a brand?

Listen to what Marty Neumeier, branding guru and Director of Transformation at Liquid Agency, has to say about it:

"A brand is a person's gut feeling about a product, service or company. It is a person's gut feeling because in the end the brand is defined by individuals, not by companies, markets or the so-called general public."

Put in terms for the short-term rental industry: your brand is how potential guests feel about the experience your rentals offer. In the end, you can't control what they think about you–but you can certainly have an impact on it.

In fact, you may have already started building your brand without even realizing it.

Do you pride your rentals on their historic charm, leading

guests to feel like they can expect a sense of nostalgia when they visit you? That will inform your brand.

Keep kid-friendly beach toys stashed in the garage, and have a colourful playroom for your little guests? That should play a part in your branding.

Building a brand from what you've got

Establishing your brand identity is a serious undertaking. Let's start small by honing in on personality—because if you don't know who you are, how can you expect potential guests to get the right idea about you?

In this section, I'll help you lay the foundation for your brand by establishing the three key personality traits of your company. I'll ask questions about your relationship with your guests, the spirit of your location, and the feeling guests get when they step foot inside your rentals to create a holistic image of your rental or business.

173

Once you've established these three traits, you can use them as your guiding light for every choice you make for your brand, from the tone of your copy to the structure of your website to the type of posts you publish on social media.

Leveraging your location identity

It goes without saying that your destination will have an impact on your brand. (You won't have much luck convincing guests to book a ski cabin in Cancun, for example.)

But one common mistake among short term rental owners and managers is relying on the location to determine a brand's entire identity.

I'm going to show you how to think about your rental(s) relationship to their location—and help you determine which aspect of your destination you should focus on to create a brand that sets you apart.

I'll also check in with John and Jane, our fictitious vacation rental managers in Cornwall, to see how they've used their property's location to their advantage.

Ready to get started? Let's kick it off by zooming out to the big picture.

What is your destination known for?

Take a second and make a list of the reasons why people visit your destination—not necessarily your rental specifically, but your city/town or community. Are you in the heart of wine country? Next to sugar-sand beaches? Do people come to eat delicious cuisine? To tour museums? To hike trails through old-growth trees? Are they coming for exhibitions, popular landmarks or is it near a beach?

Really dig down as far into specifics as you can. "To explore the outdoors" is pretty general. Better to say something like, "to ski world-class trails at the resorts," or "to snorkel on the reef."

If you're in a well-known destination, your work is a little easier at this step. But if you're a bit off the beaten path, work doubly hard to identify every reason why your town is one worth visiting.

Once you've gotten the big picture, it's time to get specific.

luxury short term rental in Hampshire

How do your rentals fit into your destination?

In the last step, you probably came to the conclusion that there's a lot to love about your destination. In this step, you're going to figure out what *you* have to offer for the folks that already love your corner of the world.

Go through your list and choose **one item that your rental uniquely allows guests to experience.**

Maybe you're a certified foodie who has connections at local restaurants (or exceptional dishes to recommend). Maybe guests can walk out your front door and onto a great hiking trail. These are your way in!

We're not saying that guests won't be able to enjoy *every* aspect of your location when they visit—of course they can. But if you speak to too broad of an audience, you risk appearing as if you don't understand the needs or wants of those your rental is best suited for.

How do you stand apart from your neighbours?

The key here is to really think about why/how you're better than your neighbours.

If you've chosen to highlight your close proximity to the beaches, how is staying at your home a better way to enjoy the beach than staying at the home next door? Are you fully stocked with beach toys and towels, perhaps? Is your home designed to maximise ocean views?

Note for property managers: If you have several homes in various places in the area, you can still have a local focus.

Think about how your standard amenities and hosting cater to your destination. Like that aforementioned collection of beach goodies, for example. Or your decades of knowledge about which beaches are best.

John & Jane's Location Identity

Let's take a look at John and Jane, our fictitious owners of beach cottages in Cornwall.

Together, with input from their past guests, they came up with a list of reasons why people visit Cornwall, including:

- Visit the beaches
- Go to festivals
- Photography
- Shop and visit galleries downtown
- Surfing/sailing events
- Attend a wedding
- Fishing and seafood

While different guests have visited for every reason on the list, their cottages 'proximity to Eden Project, the iconic eco park and educational centre leads them to choosing photography and beaches as their focus

But how can they set themselves apart from other nearby rentals?

John and Jane's brand should incorporate their proximity to, and knowledge of, the Eden Project. Social media posts and newsletter content should provide unique insight into the area's history, and design—including the logo—should incorporate some elements of elegance as a nod to the Land's End Attraction landmark. Consider including references to the galleries when naming properties, and tie the history of the area into the brand story.

Expressing your property personality

We've talked about you, the host/ property manager/ operator. We've talked about location. Finally, let's talk about what your guests are actually booking—the space.

The homes/ properties you choose, and the way you appoint them, say a lot about your values. It's your mission to reflect those same values in your branding through content and design.

In this section, I'll pick your brain to figure out the vibe of your rentals to help you start appealing to guests on an emotional level via your brand.

Let's kick off by thinking about your guests.

How do you want guests to feel when they're in your space?

No doubt you've spent a lot of time considering the design and appointments of your property, but have you stopped to think about how guests *feel* when they walk in the front door? Or when they sit down for meals, tuck in at night, or greet the morning?

All short term rental owners and managers want their guests to feel at ease, but there's a difference between the kick-off-your-boots comfort you'll find in front of a cabin's fireplace and the treat-yourself indulgence you'd expect of a penthouse in London.

How does your space–including its design, features, and amenities–instruct your guests to feel? If you're having a hard time answering this question, it might be because you know your property too well. Ask some friends–or better yet, past guests–for their responses.

How do guests use your space?

The way you speak to, interact with, and present your properties to guests *must* take into account how they plan on using your space.

High-end homes that attract special events and discerning clientele need to prove that they take guest experiences very seriously. Likewise, family retreats should convey a sense of warm welcome. Branding can help properties across the spectrum convey the right message and attract the right guests.

Through your design, voice, and communications you can subtly show guests what your space is best equipped for– whether it's a romantic and elegant web design that appeals to brides-to-be searching for their dream venue, or wanderlust-inspiring social media posts that steal the hearts of explorers seeking a home base for their adventures.

How does your rental fit in with its surroundings?

In the last section we talked about leveraging your location into part of your branding. Here, we're considering your immediate surroundings—like the community your properties are a part of, or the serene acreage they're set on.

Surroundings are often just as diverse as rentals themselves, but here are some strategies I've found helpful for the most common situations I've seen among the owners and property managers I've worked with.

1. If your homes are located in a resort community, consider its brand when building your own. What elements of the resort experience are reflected in your rentals?

2. If there's something truly unconventional about your surroundings—like if it's set on a working farm or secluded desert—make that uniqueness work for you by incorporating it into your identity.

3. If you have a collection of properties that share land, work on building a cohesive brand for the group, but also think about how each rental is different.

4. If your surroundings are run-of-the-mill in a dense town or city, don't fret! Focus on your location instead.

Search Engine Optimisation

Search engine optimisation (SEO) is one of the most debated online marketing techniques in our industry. That's because its efficacy is hard to prove, and techniques have to constantly change to outmanoeuvre Google's updates. Google maintains strict control and secrecy about how they manage and update their search engine results pages. Of course, there are guidelines posted on their Webmaster Central product, and a few utterances here and there. This leaves the floor open for some serious speculation... Cue in the SEO "experts." I am not an SEO expert, nor have I played one on TV. But I am definitely a trained SEO observer who has been in the industry for a decade, and a huge fan of web analytics and data-driven decision making.

It's sad to see articles like this circulated in the short term rental industry: "Google and SEO: what you should do, should not do, penguin, panic, panda, algorithm," followed by "please hire us, we have the answer." These articles are usually written by the SEO Manager of a big WalMart-style hotel marketing agency. Agencies also circulate baseless, misleading and ridiculous statistics, like: "56% of hotel revenue is from SEO."

On the other side, there is a counter-culture saying that SEO is dead and has been dead for a while. Both camps are wrong. Extreme views and made-up statistics like these are harmful to the hotel and short term rental industry.

So, when did it all get out of hand? What should serviced apartment brands and travel websites really be doing to improve their Google organic (SEO) revenue? Let's start by taking a look back ...way back.

The Golden Age of Hotel SEO/Remember the Titans?

There was a Golden Age of accommodation SEO? You better believe it! It was 2000-2010. I vividly remember it. A hotel could not only get placement right on the very top left of the screen for hyper-competitive terms like "hotels in Birmingham" or "hotels in London," but could also get hundreds of thousands of visits and millions of pounds in revenue. There were no maps, no carousels, and no hotel finders.

Now guess who really capitalised on SEO during this Golden Age. If you guessed hotel brands, you are wrong. OTAs like Expedia.com and Hotels.com ruled in the US; Booking.com in Europe made millions. (Their success continues to this day.) Brands like Hilton, Marriott, Starwood and IHG, to name a few, were actually busy shutting down their property-level websites. Hotel marketing types refused to believe in online marketing; they were so caught up in their own hype that they missed the boat to the greatest hotel revenue party on the planet. It was a blunder that is painful for me to bring up, but for the sake of history I must.

Fast forward to today. OTAs still rule Google and rank for some heavy-hitting terms. However, Google any "hotel + city name" term and you will no longer see an independent hotel, or a brand site, show up on the top half of your screen. Google has taken a machete to the traditional organic results page to push the products that make them money. Now it's all about the Benjamins (Google Map Ads,

Google Hotel Ads, and good old PPC).

2020 might not be the Golden Age of Hotel SEO, but there is much you can do. "Optimise everything" is my philosophy. Here are some things you need to consider if you are serious about improving your brand's website's organic rankings and online revenue.

1. Open Source or Bust

Owning your brand is bigger then SEO, always has been and always will be. There is one real estate market that is booming in marketing land: it's called **making and owning your brand**. Renting your brand website from channel managers or platforms like Wix or Lodgify- − your most profitable direct revenue channel − needs to be dropped like a bad habit (or hot potato, you choose). Don't give away the keys to your online home by building it on a closed proprietary CMS (content management system) that you can't control, remove or optimise at will.

Instead, get a cool design from ThemeForest and then pick any open source CMS (WordPress, Joomla, Drupal) to build it on. An army of developers backs these programs when it comes to Google SEO compatibility. There are also some amazing SEO plugins that will help you get back control of your SEO destiny. A lot of them tie into Google Webmaster Central and help your website maintain up-to-date Google compliance. Bonus feature: You will always own your content, photos, website and reputation. How cool is that! Double bonus: You do not lose your entire online footprint with Google every time you redesign or switch website design vendors. #winning

2. Content Is King in the Google Galaxy

There has never been a better time to invest in quality content. Accommodation and travel websites looking for organic traffic need to move away from the trend of image-rich and content-poor websites.

In case you're wondering why so many brand websites look so similar (and perform so poorly), here's the formula:

agency's website template + agency's regional sales goals + proprietary CMS + sweatshop content writers

= 1000's of zombie clone websites

Quality images are crucial for accommodation sites, but you also have to give people and search engines something nice to read. Accommodation websites stuffed with keywords and faux packages have been dropping fast since the 2011 Panda update. Updates are continuing to target websites with low-quality content. Don't let your website be average, boring and stuffed with meaningless adjectives. Participate in content generation, and say things about your apartments that really matter to your guests.

3. Aim Smaller and More Specific

You have to move beyond city name + short term rental keywords like "short term rental in Canary Wharf." Even if you rank for those keywords (good luck!), the referral traffic is diminishing rapidly.

It's time to pay attention to Latent Semantic Indexing,

which simply means that people are going to search for the same thing in different ways. Target terms travellers use to describe your brand. Why are people traveling to your location? What are they looking to do? What do they like about your property? Look into your website analytics to find out what search terms are bringing visitors to your website and your blog. Data is available to you through Google Analytics, Google Webmaster Tools and Google AdWords Keyword Tool. Please use it!

To put it another way, always try to solve a problem or answer a question for your guests. Focus on answering the questions they want answered, and you will no longer be a slave to keywords with high volume, diminishing traffic and poor conversion.

Conclusion

Search engine optimisation has been drastically transformed over the last decade. The Golden Age is over, and it will surely be missed by the providers who once made tons of revenue through higher rankings. But it's time to come to terms with current realities.

Reevaluate your SEO strategy. Are you paying for outdated services? If you're working with a larger agency, consider that they may be focused on continuing to extract profit from their well-established yet outdated SEO department. Every accommodation provider in the agency system has a big decision to make: continue paying for outdated strategies and promises by hiring "safe" and familiar vendors; or rework your search engine marketing strategy to make the most of current and future search trends.

But keep this in mind. While you sit in meetings deciding whether you want to make revenue with or without ROI reporting, Google is hustling big-time. Check out their stock price, and their online revenue from click advertising. All arrows are pointing to the sky. They want a better search page for their customers, and more ways to make money through PPC advertising and their other search products.

It's easy to get confused or caught in the middle when SEO is changing so rapidly. But no matter how much things change, it is always a good idea to move away from industrial SEO strategy and start (or continue) doing the right things: maintain control of your website, keep adding good content, blog about issues that interest your guests, build and optimise your site based on the latest techniques and technology.

As property managers and owner operators, you need to get very comfortable with the idea that you will have to continually spend money on expanding website content and buying traffic (PPC). Search changes fast, and there are no guarantees. But that doesn't mean you should feel paralysed and stop trying to make the most of your online revenue opportunities.

Chapter 7

Take advice beforehand, not afterwards.

Written by Andrew Locke LL.B(Hons) Barrister

Better to have a fence at the top of the cliff, than an ambulance at the bottom

Barristers are like dentists in many ways – not because we tell you sit down and open wide and then cause you huge amounts of pain before charging you for the pleasure – but because regular check ups and taking advice can prevent much worse problems from happening down the line. There is one major difference between law and dentistry though, and that is when someone has a problem with their teeth they generally don't have a go at sorting it out themselves, whereas with legal problems they frequently do, and get themselves into worse problems because of it.

187

When I was at Bar school one of the tutors used the following phrase which stuck with me and I have never forgotten it: "*It's a lot better to have a £500 fence at the top of the cliff than a £50,000 ambulance at the bottom*". In other words, paying a few hundred pounds to take some legal advice BEFORE you enter into a business transaction almost always works out an awful lot cheaper than going into it blind and hoping for the best, then waiting until it all goes wrong and having to pay through the nose to have it sorted out afterwards.

Many people are put off by the cost of legal advice and I am not going to deny that it is expensive, but there is a reason why lawyers charge hundreds of pounds per hour for their knowledge, advice and assistance. Law is often very complicated! What's more, contract, landlord & tenant and chancery [1] law are some of the trickiest areas and unfortunately serviced accommodation involves all of them.

The aim of this chapter is to show you a few examples of common pitfalls encountered by SME businesses generally but also with specific reference to serviced accommodation providers, landlords and agents.

Sole Trader Liability, Deadlocked Companies, Partnerships "At Will".

The first thing to decide when going into business is what legal form that business is going to take. Are you going to be a sole trader working on your own and in your own

---

[1] This includes company and partnership law, equity, trusts and land law.

name? A partnership with one or more other like minded people? Or are you going to form a company limited by shares?[2]

Many businessmen and women start out as sole traders, working on their own and perhaps also employing a couple of people, but without really thinking about the wider implications of that choice. It's often quicker and more convenient to start this way as you don't need to go through the headache of forming and registering a company, opening a separate bank account, filing company accounts etc. You can literally decide to start trading one day and be operational the next. This is often fine and causes few problems but what many people don't realise is that they are personally liable for any debts incurred or legal issues encountered by the business. Given that Rent to Rent (R2R) deals are often of long duration (3 or 5 year leases seem to be the norm) and of substantial value over the term of the lease (six figures is not uncommon), the potential downside is obvious and enormous and we are talking about "lose your house" levels of exposure if something goes wrong. If, however, the business had been structured as a limited liability company, unless the dispute involves one of those very rare instances of "lifting the corporate veil", the owner(s) (the shareholders) and those who run the company (the directors) are protected from personal liability.

That is not to say forming a company and then running your business through it is without its complications as

---

[2] There are other forms of companies and partnerships but they are nowhere near as common and discussion of them is beyond the scope of this chapter .

many small business owners do not understand the special legal nature of a limited company or their role within it. All too often people get their accountant to set up a company for them and start trading without taking any legal advice and without realising that the company has a legal status and existence of its own and has rights and duties which are separate to those of the directors and shareholders. And likewise, the directors have a set of quite onerous duties towards the company and, in certain circumstances, can be sued by it. Many small business "owners" wear at least two hats where they are both a director and shareholder of the company, although sometimes they might only be a director but not a shareholder or they might be a shareholder but not a director. Problems often arise when they have not understood the different roles they are performing and have muddied the waters in such a way that these roles have come into conflict with each other.

When advising small businesses one of the other most common problems I encounter is the deadlocked company. This is usually where 2 people (often friends, or husband and wife) form a company where they are equal shareholders and each of them is a director. When things are going well this is not an issue, but if there is a falling out or one of them simply wants to take the company in a different direction, because each of them has equal voting rights (either in a shareholders 'meeting or a board meeting) neither of them can get a decision passed unless the other agrees to it. In the absence of agreement the only way to resolve the issue is to go to court, which is eye wateringly expensive.

There are ways to avoid this situation happening and so it is important to take advice before forming a company where this is a possibility.

Similar to the deadlocked company are those businesses where two (or more) people have gone into partnership but have neglected to conclude a partnership agreement beforehand. There is nothing wrong with this per se, as partnerships do not need to have a written agreement in order to operate and if two or more people start doing business together as partners, known as "partnership at will", there is statute and case law which sets out the basic rules. However, if things go wrong somewhere down the line, often the only way to dissolve the partnership and divide the assets of the business is to go to court, which is stressful, time-consuming and very expensive. Moreover, if the partnership is not doing well, the partners remain locked together in a situation where they are both jointly and severally liable for the debts as partnerships generally do not benefit from limited liability as a company does and you end up with the worst of both worlds - the unlimited personal liability of being a sole trader and also the involvement of other people and being bound by strict legal duties[3] towards them which you get when you form a company.

The Importance of Well Drafted Contracts

I find myself writing this during the Covid 19 lockdown, which has caused a sudden and very sharp downturn in the market for all businesses, but especially those in the

---

[3] Known as "fiduciary duties"

hospitality and letting sectors. I have advised a number of businesses (including SA operators) and have been shocked to find that not only are many of the contracts, tenancy agreements and leases defective but that a significant number of them haven't even committed anything to writing at all!

By far the biggest problem is that many of the leases and tenancy agreements are drafted as Assured Shorthold Tenancies when they are not or even if they are not, the terms have clearly just been copied and pasted from one. Unlike Ronseal, tenancy agreements do not always do what they say on the tin[4]. Just because a document may be entitled "Assured Shorthold Tenancy", it will not be an AST unless a specific set of factual criteria apply, primarily that the tenant is a "natural person", ie: a human being, and that the property is used as the tenant's only or principal home. R2R leases never fulfil this criteria as the "tenant" (the SA operator) is often a company and even if they are not, they are not using the property as their only or principal home. Also, the tenancy deposit protection provisions contained in the Housing Act 2004 do not apply but many agreements unnecessarily and potentially problematically incorporate some or all of the the statutory requirements.

Problems are not confined to the tenancy agreements. In their (understandable) eagerness to get on with the business of making money many people go into deals with their customers or suppliers without properly concluding a contract where all the necessary terms of the deal are

---

[4] Or, as Lord Bingham said in *Antoniades v Villiers* [1990] 1 AC 417, CA: "A cat does not become a dog just because the parties have agreed to call it a dog"

clear. This can range from "battle of the forms" type situations where both parties have exchanged their standard terms and conditions, often by email and often without other party reading them, or where they have simply agreed to do something and then only later have received terms and conditions (eg: printed on the back of a receipt or acknowledgment of an order). Sometimes the terms of the agreement have to be gleaned from examining long chains of email correspondence going back months and months. And sometimes there simply have been no written terms and conditions exchanged, even in some very big deals – I once advised in case where almost £300,000 worth of custom made machinery had been ordered without any written terms being agreed! The absence of a written document entitled "Contract" or "Terms and Conditions" does not mean there is no contract between the parties as contracts do not need to be in writing (unless it is for the sale of land) and so in the event of a dispute it can be the devil's own job to work out who was supposed to do what and when and for how much. And guess who benefits from these sort of disputes where there is uncertainty? Yes. It is us lawyers, because business people end up having to pay us lots and lots of money to try and sort it all out.

Final Word: Keep Your Eyes Open and Your Mouth Shut.

"Sticks and stones may break my bones but words will never hurt me"

Wrong. If you put them on FaceBook they might.

Social media is increasingly used by businesses as a shop window and marketing tool. However, perhaps because of its origins in building online friendship and family groups, many people treat social media as if they were having a private conversation when in fact it is much more akin to publishing a newspaper article or a book. Everything you post on social media is potentially permanent and something said out of turn can easily come back to bite you.

Last year I represented a well known serviced accommodation operator and trainer in High Court defamation (libel) proceedings after a business rival rather unwisely made some scurrilous and wholly unfounded accusations about him on FaceBook. The case settled in my client's favour but not before it cost the guy on the other side a lot of time, effort and money, not to mention pride as part of the settlement was that he had to post an apology online.

Such comments (or unfair and factually incorrect online reviews) can be incredibly harmful to a business which relies on the internet for its presence and referrals, so it is a very good idea to regularly check for such material.

So, if you do get involved in an online spat with a keyboard warrior, before posting your response, it may be wise to take a deep breath and step away from the computer.....

About Andrew Locke

Andrew Locke is a barrister specialising in commercial and landlord & tenant/ housing law.

He practises from Nexus, The Chambers of Michael Mansfield QC and also runs a telephone legal advice service, "the legal lifeLine"

This chapter above was adapted from a series of blogs which were published on the legal lifeLine website: www.thelegallifeline.co.uk

Final Thoughts

How to create business equity and competitive advantage with your client list

There is little real equity and no security in the assets bankers look at on balance sheets and that most business owners price, like patents,

trademarks, buildings, equipment or inventory - because it's all worthless without customers and customers in development. The true equity is in client/ guest lists.

Further, most business owners live with utter uncertainty and insecurity

day by day, only presuming or hoping people will arrive and buy or

book, but as the financial people constantly caution: past gains are not predictive or future results. To be in control you must have well-kept, ready to use client lists including email and physical addresses.

Any business that isn't ALWAYS list building is failing. Think about it for a second, if you could have one thing from one of the biggest SA operators or Corporate travel agents in the country, what would it be? It would be their client list right? Because it's so valuable, they guard it with everything they have! Repeat clients and clients that

refer you to other clients are the best sort of clients to have. They can literally make you millions of pounds without spending too much on advertising. But don't be fooled, the big operators knew this from

inception, that's why they're so far ahead. List building was part of their strategy right from the beginning, and the hard work is paying off.

So whatever you do, from today, implement a list building strategy for your brand.

Nurture those lists, and you'll see your revenue increase & outgoings stabilise year on year.

Good luck and best wishes!
Emilia

Index of acronyms you might come across:

STR- short term rentals

ADR- average daily rate

GHA- Google hotel ads

SEO- search engine optimisation

BDC- booking.com

OTA- online travel agent

CRM- customer relationship management

BRA- best rates available

DB- direct bookings

IBE- internet booking engine

Rack rate- the normal price for a room/ apartment prior to any discounts.

Serviced Apartments- long stay accommodation that often includes cleaning but tends to be self catering where meals are not included.

LM- last minute guest who comes to stay within 72 hours of booking.

WI- a guest who comes to stay with no prior booking.

PMS- property management system

RevPAR- revenue per available room

NOI- net operating income

Useful resources:

Pillow Partners (SA property management)
Rentmyhouse.co.uk (SA management)
Matrix Consultancy Group (1:1 SA Consultancy)
Sapphire Stays (SA management)
Montauban Apartments (SA management)

Join my private Serviced Accommodation group on Facebook:

Women: 800+ members
https://www.facebook.com/groups/wsapgroup/

For everyone: 2800+ members ran by TJ Atkinson and myself
https://www.facebook.com/groups/1820378458204619

Recommendations

Channel managers:

Rentals United

Beds24 (budget friendly)

CRM:

Zendesk Sell

Agile

Accountancy:

WOW Accountancy

Legal Help:

The legal lifeLINE

Website themes:

Themeforest

Freelancers:

PPH

Fiverr

Telephone answering service:

Your Office and PA

Serviced Accommodation Business help:

Tj Atkinson- The Breakthrough

Souring R2SA properties:

Wayne Black (FB search Wayne Black property)

Property sourcing 'on-patch' training:

Ross Mallalieu (The Agent Whisperer)

The end.
Nothing for sale.

Bye!

Notes

Notes

Notes

Notes

Notes

Notes

Notes

Notes

Notes

Printed in Great Britain
by Amazon